Quotable Twain

Compiled & Edited
by
David W. Barber

Quotable Twain

Compiled & Edited
by
David W. Barber

Sound And Vision

Introduction

Samuel Langhorne Clemens (1835-1910), better known by his pen name Mark Twain, was America's first great man of letters – and indeed, he remains among the greatest writers America has ever produced. He first gained notice in November 1865 with the publication in the New York *Saturday Press* of his short story *The Celebrated Jumping Frog of Calavaras County*, a folksy tale of a swindler. He went on to earn worldwide renown for *Tom Sawyer* and its sequel, *Huckleberry Finn* – adventure stories ostensibly for children but also admired and enjoyed by adults – for such memoirs and travelogues as *Life on the Mississippi* and *The Innocents Abroad*, and for such satirical works as the genial *A Connecticut Yankee in King Arthur's Court* and the more sharply cynical *Letters from the Earth* (reports from Satan on the progress of God's little "experiment," a work considered too controversial to have been published in Twain's lifetime).

Twain was a prolific and versatile craftsman who worked in virtually every medium available to a 19th-century writer: novels, non-fiction books, short stories, newspaper and magazine articles, essays, letters, pamphlets and, especially as his reputation and fame grew, in public lectures and speeches. If he were still alive today, you can be sure he'd have expanded his outlets to include radio, TV, the Internet and – who knows? – probably online newsgroups. Twain was a sucker for new technology, and lost considerable money investing in a new printing press. He also bought one of the first typewriters, invented by Christopher Scholes, the Remington I. But he could never get the hang of it and later gave it to his friend and editor, William Dean Howells. Twain was the first writer to submit a typewritten manuscript to his publisher (though he didn't type it, an assistant did from his longhand notes). In his memoirs, Twain says it was *Tom Sawyer*, but he remembered incorrectly. Diligent research by the typewriter historian Darryl Rehr shows it was in fact *Life on the Mississippi*, published in 1883.

Twain was first and foremost a writer – although along the way he'd tried his hand at many things besides. He began as a typesetter's apprentice and became a printer, at a newspaper owned by his older brother, Orion Clemens. He spent a few years piloting steamboats on the Mississippi River. Piloting was a vocation at which he was quite capable – none of his customers ever lost goods or suffered damage when he was at the wheel – one he loved and one he often longed to return to. The river is at the heart of his memoir *Life on the Mississippi* and also forms a central plot element – Huck and the slave Jim's escape on a raft – in *Huckleberry Finn*. River piloting is also generally thought to have been the origin of his pen name, where the call of "mark twain!" signifies a depth of two fathoms, or 12 feet, which is deep enough to navigate (though some contrarian Twain scholars have suggested the name comes from the number of drinks chalked up on a Nevada saloon tab).

When the Civil War blocked river traffic in 1861, Twain was forced to abandon piloting. As a Southerner, he felt obliged to sign on to the Confederate side. His career as a soldier lasted about two weeks, before the rag-tag company he'd joined fell apart. He was a miserable recruit ("I could have become a soldier if I had waited," he writes in *The Private History of a Campaign That Failed*. "I knew more about retreating than the man who invented retreating.") and anyway, his heart wasn't in it. (In a speech in 1881, he dismissed war as "a wanton waste of projectiles.")

For the remainder of the war, he scrambled to write journalism and later tried his hand mining for gold and silver in Nevada, where Orion had accepted a job as assistant to the territorial governor. It was in Nevada that Twain later accepted his first full-time newspaper job, as city editor of the Nevada *Territorial Enterprise*. (It was a wise choice: The mining didn't exactly pan out.)

Twain's varied life experience, coupled with his keen wit and a deep sense of irony – not to mention his renown – make him of course eminently quotable. So quotable, in fact, that many witty or pithy expressions (such as "The man who does not read good books has no advantage over the man who can't read them," or "Wagner's music is better than it sounds," in which Twain was knowingly quoting another humorist, Bill Nye) are attributed to him whether he actually said them or not. Others, such as his celebrated "reports of my death" quote, have been embellished and improved upon (both the quote itself and the story surrounding it) and burnished to such a sheen that it's sometimes hard to determine what Twain actually did say – if indeed he said anything of the sort. Twain himself, of course, knew this, knew that a well-turned phrase was worth its weight in gold (as a failed prospector, Twain knew something of gold's value), and knew that quotations and expressions sometimes take on a life, and a currency, of their own beyond whoever said them. ("It is my belief," he writes in *Following the Equator*, "that nearly any invented quotation, played with confidence, stands a good chance to deceive.")

As a journalist and a writer, Twain hated censorship and extolled the value of free speech. It's ironic, then, that some of his works – particularly *Huckleberry Finn*, for its casual use of the term "nigger" – should fall victim to high-minded censors, even in his own day, as much as our own. But Twain was a writer of his time with a keen ear for dialect and dialogue, and "nigger" was a term very much in use in the mid-19th century. It seems to be no use explaining to such zealots that Huck himself never uses the term derisively, or that the whole point of the story is Huck's attempts to help a black man, Jim, escape from slavery. Was Mark Twain a racist? Hardly. Indeed, for a white man who grew up in (relative) comfort in the American South of before and after the Civil War, Twain was remarkably tolerant and accepting of other races, religions and viewpoints. In 1885, Twain met Warner T. McGuinn, one of the first black students admitted to Yale Law School, and offered to help pay his living expenses, as a way of helping the black cause (and maybe a little in guilt over the South's history of slavery). In a letter to Francis Wayland, dean of the Yale Law School, he writes: "We have ground the manhood out of them, & the shame is ours, not theirs, & we should pay for it." Twain also offered to financially help another black student, but that student did not enroll.

Although best known as a humorist, Twain also became a keen observer and an insightful, sometimes cynical, commentator on the foibles of human nature and human society – often, of course, mixing the two for best effect. ("If you pick up a starving dog and make him prosperous, he will not bite you," he writes in *Pudd'nhead Wilson's Calendar*. "This is the principal difference between a dog and a man.") Like many humorists, Twain's personal life was tinged with tragedy. He and his beloved wife, Olivia Langdon Clemens (who was ill for much of their marriage), had four children – a son and three daughters. But their son, Langdon, born prematurely, died before his second birthday, and two daughters died in their 20s, Susy at 23 and Jean at 29. Their middle daughter, Clara, lived to the ripe old age of 88.

It was the tragedy of these deaths, and other misfortunes, I'm sure, that brought out Twain's jaded, dark side. This is never more evident than in that remarkably progressive and provocative book, *Letters from the Earth*, in which, through the voice of Satan, he attacks the foolishness of Christianity and the hypocrisy of the God of the Bible ("It does not appear that [God] ever stopped to reflect that he was to blame when a man went wrong," Satan writes in *Letter X*, "inasmuch as the man was merely acting in accordance with the disposition he had afflicted him with.") Twain wrote the work in 1909, the year before his death in 1910. But his daughter Clara kept a tight control of his literary estate, particularly guarding this manuscript, letters and other material that she felt portrayed Twain as anything other than the jovial, charming gentleman. It wasn't until after her death in 1962 that *Letters from the Earth* could be published. Even today, nearly a century after it was written, it remains a startlingly progressive and remarkable work.

Many people picture Mark Twain as the genial Southern gentleman dressed in a white suit, with a shock of white hair and luxuriant moustache, smoking a big cigar (or sometimes a pipe) and dispensing witty sayings and pithy observations. All of which is true, though it was an image, later in life, he was careful to cultivate for public consumption. He was born with red – or, as he might say – auburn hair, which went white as he aged. In later life, he kept a closetful of those white suits, and probably a drawerful of cigars, as much for the persona, I'm sure, as for the enjoyment. ("I never smoke to excess," he said in his 1909 speech *Advice to Girls*, at 73 his last public appearance, "that is, I smoke in moderation, only one cigar at a time.")

There's much to enjoy in the writings of Mark Twain, and even much to learn from him. Above all, let's remember his advice in *Puddn'head Wilson's Calendar*: "Let us endeavor so to live that when we come to die even the undertaker will be sorry."

DWB
Toronto, Canada, 2002

ACTORS

... the ordinary run of newspaper criticism will not do to depend upon. ... Pay no attention to the papers, but watch the audience.
— *Answers to Correspondents, Californian* (1865)

ADAM

It all began with Adam. He was the first man to tell a joke – or a lie. How lucky Adam was. He knew when he said a good thing, nobody had said it before. Adam was not alone in the Garden of Eden, however, and does not deserve all the credit; much is due to Eve, the first woman, and Satan, the first consultant.
— *Notebook*, 1867

It was not that Adam ate the apple for the apple's sake, but because it was forbidden. It would have been better for us – oh infinitely better for us – if the serpent had been forbidden.
— *Notebook*

Adam was but human – this explains it all. He did not want the apple for the apple's sake, he wanted it only because it was forbidden. The mistake was in not forbidding the serpent; then he would have eaten the serpent.
— *Pudd'nhead Wilson*

Adam and Eve had many advantages, but the principal one was that they escaped teething.
— *Pudd'nhead Wilson's Calendar*

Let us be thankful to Adam our benefactor. He cut us out of the "blessing" of idleness and won for us the "curse" of labor.
— *Following the Equator*

After all these years, I see that I was mistaken about Eve in the beginning; it is better to live outside the Garden with her than inside it without her.
— *Adam's Diary*

ADJECTIVES

As to the Adjective: When in doubt, strike it out.
– Pudd'nhead Wilson

You need not expect to get your book right the first time. Go to work and revamp or rewrite it. God only exhibits his thunder and lightning at intervals, and so they always command attention. These are God's adjectives. You thunder and lightning too much; the reader ceases to get under the bed, by and by.
– Letter to Orion Clemens, 1878

I notice that you use plain, simple language, short words and brief sentences. That is the way to write English – it is the modern way and the best way. Stick to it; don't let fluff and flowers and verbosity creep in. When you catch an adjective, kill it. No, I don't mean utterly, but kill most of them – then the rest will be valuable. They weaken when they are close together. They give strength when they are wide apart. An adjective habit, or a wordy, diffuse, flowery habit, once fastened upon a person, is as hard to get rid of as any other vice.
– Letter to D. W. Bowser, Mar. 20, 1880

ADULTERY

Thou shalt not commit adultery is a command which makes no distinction between the following persons. They are all required to obey it: children at birth. Children in the cradle. School children. Youths and maidens. Fresh adults. Older ones. Men and women of 40. Of 50. Of 60. Of 70. Of 80. Of 100. The command does not distribute its burden equally, and cannot. It is not hard upon the three sets of children.
– Satan's Letter VIII, Letters from the Earth

ADVERSITY

By trying we can easily learn to endure adversity – another man's I mean.
– Following the Equator

ADVERTISING

Many a small thing has been made large by the right kind of advertising.
— A Connecticut Yankee in King Arthur's Court

ADVICE

There are three things which I consider excellent advice. First, don't smoke to excess. Second, don't drink to excess. Third, don't marry to excess.
— Last public address, St. Timothy's School for Girls, Catonsville, MY, 1909

You should never do anything wicked and lay it on your brother, when it is just as convenient to lay it on some other boy.
— Advice for Good Little Boys

Be respectful to your superiors, if you have any.
— Advice to Young People speech, 1882

AGE

You can't reach old age by another man's road. My habits protect my life but they would assassinate you.
— 70th Birthday speech, 1905

Wrinkles should merely indicate where the smiles have been.
— Following the Equator

Life would be infinitely happier if we could only be born at the age of eighty and gradually approach eighteen.
— quoted in Autobiography with Letters, William L. Phelps

What ought to be done to the man who invented the celebrating of anniversaries? Mere killing would be too light.
— Noteboook, 1896

I was young and foolish then; now I am old and foolisher.
— Mark Twain, a Biography

AMERICA

We are called the nation of inventors. And we are. We could still claim that title and wear its loftiest honors if we had stopped with the first thing we ever invented, which was human liberty.

– Foreign Critics speech, 1890

ANGER

When angry count four; when very angry, swear.

– Pudd'nhead Wilson's Calendar

ANSWERS

I was gratified to be able to answer promptly, and I did. I said I didn't know.

– Life on the Mississippi

APRIL FOOLS DAY

This is the day upon which we are reminded of what we are on the other three hundred and sixty-four.

– Pudd'nhead Wilson's Calendar

APPROVAL

We can secure other people's approval if we do right and try hard; but our own is worth a hundred of it, and no way has been found out of securing that.

– Following the Equator

ARCHITECTS

Architects cannot teach nature anything.

– Memorable Midnight Experience

ARISTOCRACY

Any kind of royalty, however modified, any kind of aristocracy, however pruned, is rightly an insult.

– A Connecticut Yankee in King Arthur's Court

ART

I am glad the old masters are all dead, and I only wish they had died sooner.
> – *Academy of Design*, letter to San Francisco
> *Alta California*, July 28, 1867

ASTRONOMY

I love to revel in philosophical matters – especially astronomy. I study astronomy more than any other foolishness there is.
> – *Letter from Mark Twain*, San Francisco
> *Alta California*, Aug. 1, 1869

AUSTEN, JANE

Jane Austen? Why I go so far as to say that any library is a good library that does not contain a volume by Jane Austen. Even if it contains no other book.
> – Quoted in *Remembered Yesterdays*, Robert Underwood Johnson

I haven't any right to criticize books, and I don't do it except when I hate them. I often want to criticize Jane Austen, but her books madden me so that I can't conceal my frenzy from the reader; and therefore I have to stop every time I begin. Every time I read *Pride and Prejudice* I want to dig her up and beat her over the skull with her own shin-bone.
> – Letter to Joseph Twichell, Sept. 13, 1898

To me [Edgar Allan Poe's] prose is unreadable – like Jane Austin's [sic]. No there is a difference. I could read his prose on salary, but not Jane's. Jane is entirely impossible. It seems a great pity that they allowed her to die a natural death.
> – Letter to W. D. Howells, Jan, 18, 1909

AUTHORS

I have been an author for 20 years and an ass for 55.
> – *Mark Twain, a Biography*

An author values a compliment even when it comes from a source of doubtful competency.

– Autobiography of Mark Twain

BABIES

Sufficient unto the day is one baby. As long as you are in your right mind don't you ever pray for twins. Twins amount to a permanent riot; and there ain't any real difference between triplets and an insurrection.

– Babies speech, 1879

A baby is an inestimable blessing and bother.

– Letter to Annie Webster, 1876

BEAUTY

There are women who have an indefinable charm in their faces which makes them beautiful to their intimates, but a cold stranger who tried to reason the matter out and find this beauty would fail.

– A Tramp Abroad

BELIEF

If the man doesn't believe as we do, we say he is a crank, and that settles it. I mean, it does nowadays, because now we can't burn him.

– Following the Equator

Between believing a thing and thinking you know is only a small step and quickly taken.

– Three Thousand Years Among the Microbes

BIBLE

[The Bible] is full of interest. It has noble poetry in it; and some clever fables; and some blood-drenched history; and some good morals; and a wealth of obscenity; and upwards of a thousand lies.

– Satan's Letter III, Letters from the Earth

This Bible is built mainly out of the fragments of older Bibles that had their day and crumbled to ruin. So it noticeably lacks in originality, necessarily. Its three or four most imposing and impressive events all happened in earlier Bibles; all its best precepts and rules of conduct came also from those Bibles.

– Satan's Letter III, Letters from the Earth

When one reads Bibles, one is less surprised at what the Deity knows than at what He doesn't know.

– Notebook

BICYCLE

Get a bicycle. You will not regret it. If you live.

– Taming the Bicycle

BIERCE, AMBROSE

Bierce has written some admirable things — fugitive pieces — but none of them are 'Nuggets.' There is humor in *Dod Grile*, but for every laugh that is in his book there are five blushes, ten shudders & a vomit. The laugh is too expensive.

– Letter to Chatto and Windus, April 8, 1874

BLASPHEMY

Blasphemy? No, it is not blasphemy. If God is as vast as that, he is above blasphemy; if He is as little as that, He is beneath it.

– Mark Twain, a Biography

BLUEJAY

A bluejay hasn't any more principle than an ex-congressman, and he will steal, deceive and betray four times out of five.

– Morals lecture, July 15,1895

BLINDNESS

Blindness is an exciting business, I tell you; if you don't believe it get up some dark night on the wrong side of your bed when the house is on fire and try to find the door.

– Quoted in Midstream, Helen Keller

BOOKS

The man who does not read good books has no advantage over the man who can't read them.

– Attrib.

BOYS

We think boys are rude, insensitive animals but it is not so in all cases. Each boy has one or two sensitive spots, and if you can find out where they are located you have only to touch them and you can scorch him as with fire.

– Autobiography of Mark Twain

BRAVERY

To believe yourself brave is to be brave; it is the one only essential thing.

– Personal Recollections of Joan of Arc

BUSINESS

There are two times in a man's life when he should not speculate: when he can't afford it, and when he can.

– Following the Equator

Let your sympathies and your compassion be always with the underdog in the fight – this is magnanimity; but bet on the other one – this is business.

– Mark Twain, a Biography

CALAMITY

The calamity that comes is never the one we had prepared ourselves for.

– Letter to Olivia Clemens, Aug. 16, 1896

CATS

One of the most striking differences between a cat and a lie is that a cat has only nine lives.

– Pudd'nhead Wilson

A cat is more intelligent than people believe, and can be taught any crime.

– *Notebook*, 1895

Of all God's creatures there is only one that cannot be made the slave of the last. That one is the cat. If man could be crossed with the cat it would improve man, but it would deteriorate the cat.

– *Notebook*, 1894

I simply can't resist a cat, particularly a purring one. They are the cleanest, cunningest, and most intelligent things I know – outside of the girl you love, of course.

– Quoted in *Abroad with Mark Twain and Eugene Field*, Henry W. Fisher

CENSORSHIP

But the truth is, that when a Library expels a book of mine and leaves an unexpurgated Bible lying around where unprotected youth and age can get hold of it, the deep unconscious irony of it delights me and doesn't anger me.

– Letter to Mrs. F. G. Whitmore, Feb. 7, 1907

CHANGE

Change is the handmaiden Nature requires to do her miracles with.

– *Roughing It*

CHARACTER

One must keep one's character. Earn a character first if you can, and if you can't, then assume one. From the code of morals I have been following and revising and revising for 72 years I remember one detail. All my life I have been honest – comparatively honest. I could never use money I had not made honestly – I could only lend it.

– Speech, Dec. 22, 1907

CHARITY

In all the ages, three-fourths of the support of the great charities has been conscience money.

– A Humane Word from Satan

CHARMS

The longing of my heart is a fairy portrait of myself: I want to be pretty; I want to eliminate facts and fill up the gap with charms.

– Interview in the Seattle Star, Nov. 30, 1905

CHASTITY

Chastity – you can carry it too far.

– Mark Twain in Eruption

CHEERFULNESS

The best way to cheer yourself up is to try to cheer somebody else up.

– Notebook

A healthy and wholesome cheerfulness is not necessarily impossible to any occupation.

– The Undertaker's Chat, Sketches New and Old

CHICAGO

When you feel like tellin a feller to go to the devil – tell him to go to Chicago – it'll answer every purpose, and is perhaps, a leetle more expensive.

– Snodgrass' Ride on the Railroad, Nov. 29, 1856

CHILDREN

… what are they in the world for I don't know, for they are of no practical value as far as I can see. If I could beget a typewriter – but no, our fertile days are over.

– Letter to W. D. Howells, May 12,1899

The best minds will tell you that when a man has begotten a child he is morally bound to tenderly care for it, protect it from hurt, shield it from disease, clothe it, feed it, bear with its waywardness, lay no hand upon it save in kindness and for its own good, and never in any case inflict upon it a wanton cruelty. God's treatment of his earthly children, every day and every night, is the exact opposite of all that, yet those best minds warmly justify these crimes, condone them, excuse them, and indignantly refuse to regard them as crimes at all, when he commits them.

– *Satan's Letter III, Letters from the Earth*

CHRISTIANITY

I bring you the stately matron named Christendom, returning bedraggled, besmirched, and dishonored, from pirate raids in Kiao-Chou, Manchuria, South Africa, and the Philippines, with her soul full of meanness, her pocket full of boodle, and her mouth full of pious hypocrisies. Give her soap and towel, but hide the looking glass.

– *A Salutation from the 19th to the 20th Century,* Dec. 31, 1900

… with the serene confidence which a Christian feels in four aces.

– *Washoe – Information Wanted*

The so-called Christian nations are the most enlightened and progressive ... but in spite of their religion, not because of it. The Church has opposed every innovation and discovery from the day of Galileo down to our own time, when the use of anesthetic in childbirth was regarded as a sin because it avoided the biblical curse pronounced against Eve. And every step in astronomy and geology ever taken has been opposed by bigotry and superstition. The Greeks surpassed us in artistic culture and in architecture five hundred years before Christian religion was born.

– *Mark Twain, a Biography*

They all did their best – to kill being the chiefest ambition of the human race and the earliest incident in its history – but only the Christian civilization has scored a triumph to be proud of. Two or three centuries from now it will be recognized that all the competent killers are Christians; then the pagan world will go to school to the Christian – not to acquire his religion, but his guns.

– The Mysterious Stranger

CHURCH

The church is always trying to get other people to reform; it might not be a bad idea to reform itself a little, by way of example.

– A Tramp Abroad

Nothing agrees with me. If I drink coffee, it gives me dyspepsia; if I drink wine, it gives me the gout; if I go to church, it gives me dysentery.

– Letter to Henry H. Rogers, Aug. 7, 1905

CINCINNATI

When the end of the world comes, I want to be in Cincinnati because it's always twenty years behind the times.

– Attrib.

CIVILIZATION

Civilization is a limitless multiplication of unnecessary necessities.

– More Maxims of Mark, Merle Johnson, 1927

There is no salvation for us but to adopt Civilization and lift ourselves down to its level.

– To the Person Sitting in Darkness

There are many humorous things in the world; among them, the white man's notion that he is less savage than the other savages.

– Following the Equator

Every civilization carries the seeds of its own destruction, and the same cycle shows in them all. The Republic is born, flourishes, decays into plutocracy, and is captured by the shoemaker whom the mercenaries and millionaires make into a king. The people invent their oppressors, and the oppressors serve the function for which they are invented.

– Mark Twain in Eruption

My idea of our civilization is that it is a shoddy, poor thing and full of cruelties, vanities, arrogances, meannesses and hypocrisies.

– Mark Twain, a Biography

CLOTHES

Clothes make the man. Naked people have little or no influence in society.

– Quoted in More Maxims of Mark, Merle Johnson, 1927

COLD

Cold! If the thermometer had been an inch longer we'd all have frozen to death.

– Quoted in Mark Twain and I, Opie Read

Shut the door. Not that it lets in the cold but that it lets out the coziness.

– Notebook, 1898

COMMUNISM

Communism is idiocy. They want to divide up the property. Suppose they did it – it requires brains to keep money as well as make it. In a precious little while the money would be back in the former owner's hands and the communist would be poor again.

– Mark Twain, a Biography

COMPLIMENT

I have been complimented many times and they always embarrass me; I always feel that they have not said enough.

– Speech, Sept. 23, 1907

CONFESSIONAL

The confessional's chief amusement has been seduction – in all the ages of the Church.

– Satan's Letter XI, Letters from the Earth

CONFORMITY

Whenever you find yourself on the side of the majority, it is time to reform (or pause and reflect).

– Notebook, 1904

CONGRESS

It could probably be shown by facts and figures that there is no distinctly native American criminal class except Congress.

– Following the Equator

... I never can think of Judas Iscariot without losing my temper. To my mind Judas Iscariot was nothing but a low, mean, premature, Congressman.

– Foster's Case, New York Tribune, March 10,1873

Fleas can be taught nearly anything that a Congressman can.

– What is Man? and Other Essays, 1917

CONSCIENCE

Good friends, good books and a sleepy conscience: this is the ideal life.

– Notebook; also in More Maxims of Mark, Merle Johnson, 1927

CONSPIRACY

The wronger a conspiracy is, the better it is.

– Tom Sawyer's Conspiracy

COOPER, JAMES FENIMORE

[Editor's note: There's no doubt Twain could be acerbic – nasty, even – about many things, including other writers. (See for instance his remarks on Jane Austen, above.) But never was he more caustic – or funnier – than in his attack on the writing of James Fenimore Cooper

(1789-1851), creator of the *Leatherstocking Tales,* including *The Deerslayer, The Last of the Mohicans* and *The Pathfinder,* and their frontiersman hero with the unlikely name of Natty Bumpo, a.k.a. "Hawkeye." Twain opens his essay *Fenimore Cooper's Literary Offences* by quoting a couple of esteemed literature professors, one from Yale, one from Columbia, and the novelist Wilkie Collins to the effect that, as Collins puts it, Cooper is "the greatest artist in the domain of romantic fiction yet produced by America." Unable to stand it any longer, Twain launches in. Here's an abbreviated version:]

It seems to me that it was far from right for [these men] to deliver opinions on Cooper's literature without having read some of it. It would have been much more decorous to keep silent and let persons talk who have read Cooper.

Cooper's art has some defects. In one place in *Deerslayer,* and in the restricted space of two-thirds of a page, Cooper has scored 114 offenses against literary art out of a possible 115. It breaks the record.

There are nineteen rules governing literary art in the domain of romantic fiction – some say twenty-two. In *Deerslayer* Cooper violated eighteen of them. These eighteen require:

• That a tale shall accomplish something and arrive somewhere. But the *Deerslayer* tale accomplishes nothing and arrives in the air.

• They require that the episodes of a tale shall be necessary parts of the tale, and shall help to develop it. But as the *Deerslayer* tale is not a tale, and accomplishes nothing and arrives nowhere, the episodes have no rightful place in the work, since there was nothing for them to develop.

• They require that the personages in a tale shall be alive, except in the case of corpses, and that always the reader shall be able to tell the corpses from the others. But this detail has often been overlooked in the *Deerslayer* tale.

• They require that the personages in a tale, both dead and alive, shall exhibit a sufficient excuse for being there. But this detail also has been overlooked in the *Deerslayer* tale.

• They require that when the personages of a tale deal in conversation, the talk shall sound like human talk, and be talk such as human beings would be likely to talk in the given circumstances, and have a discoverable meaning, also a discoverable purpose, and a show of relevancy, and remain in the neighborhood of the subject in hand, and be interesting to the reader, and help out the tale, and stop when the people cannot think of anything more to say. But this requirement has been ignored from the beginning of the *Deerslayer* tale to the end of it.

• They require that when the author describes the character of a personage in his tale, the conduct and conversation of that personage shall justify said description. But this law gets little or no attention in the *Deerslayer* tale, as Natty Bumpo's case will amply prove.

• They require that when a personage talks like an illustrated, gilt-edged, tree-calf, hand-tooled, seven-dollar *Friendship's Offering* in the beginning of a paragraph, he shall not talk like a negro minstrel in the end of it. But this rule is flung down and danced upon in the *Deerslayer* tale.

• They require that crass stupidities shall not be played upon the reader as "the craft of the woodsman, the delicate art of the forest," by either the author or the people in the tale. But this rule is persistently violated in the *Deerslayer* tale.

• They require that the personages of a tale shall confine themselves to possibilities and let miracles alone; or, if they venture a miracle, the author must so plausibly set it forth as to make it look possible or reasonable. But these rules are not respected in the *Deerslayer* tale.

• They require that the author shall make the reader feel a deep interest in the personages of his tale and in their fate; and that he shall make the reader love the good people in the tale and hate the bad ones. But the reader of the *Deerslayer* tale dislikes the good people in it, is indifferent to the others, and wishes they would all get drowned together.

• They require that the characters in a tale shall be so clearly defined that the reader can tell beforehand what each will do in a given emergency. But in the *Deerslayer* tale this rule is vacated.

In addition to these large rules there are some little ones. These require that the author shall

• Say what he is proposing to say, not merely come near it.
• Use the right word, not its second cousin.
• Eschew surplusage.
• Not omit necessary details.

Quotable Twain

- Avoid slovenliness of form.
- Use good grammar.
- Employ a simple and straightforward style.

Even these seven are coldly and persistently violated in the *Deerslayer* tale.

Cooper's gift in the way of invention was not a rich endowment; but such as it was he liked to work it, he was pleased with the effects, and indeed he did some quite sweet things with it. In his little box of stage-properties he kept six or eight cunning devices, tricks, artifices for his savages and woodsmen to deceive and circumvent each other with, and he was never so happy as when he was working these innocent things and seeing them go. A favorite one was to make a moccasined person tread in the tracks of the moccasined enemy, and thus hide his own trail. Cooper wore out barrels and barrels of moccasins in working that trick. Another stage-property that he pulled out of his box pretty frequently was his broken twig. He prized his broken twig above all the rest of his effects, and worked it the hardest.

It is a restful chapter in any book of his when somebody doesn't step on a dry twig and alarm all the reds and whites for two hundred yards around. Every time a Cooper person is in peril, and absolute silence is worth four dollars a minute, he is sure to step on a dry twig. There may be a hundred handier things to step on, but that wouldn't satisfy Cooper. Cooper requires him to turn out and find a dry twig; and if he can't do it, go and borrow one. In fact, the *Leatherstocking Series* ought to have been called the *Broken Twig Series*. ...

If Cooper had any real, knowledge of Nature's way of doing things, he had a most delicate art in concealing the fact. For instance: one of his acute Indian experts, Chingachgook (pronounced Chicago, I think), has lost the trail of a person he is tracking through the forest. Apparently the trail is hopelessly lost. Neither you or I could ever have guessed out the way to find it. It was very different with Chicago. Chicago was not stumped for long. He turned a running stream out of its course, and there, in the slush in its old bed, were that person's moccasin tracks. The current did not wash them away, as it would have done in all other like cases – no, even the eternal laws of Nature have to vacate when Cooper wants to put up a delicate job of woodcraft on the reader. …

Cooper seldom saw anything correctly. He saw nearly all things as through a glass eye, darkly. …Cooper is not a close observer, but he is interesting. He is certainly always that, no matter what happens. And he is more interesting when he is not noticing what he is about than when he is. This is a considerable merit.

The conversations in the Cooper books have a curious sound in our modern ears. To believe that such talk really ever came out of people's mouths would be to believe that there was a time when time was of no value to a person who thought he had something to say; when it was the custom to spread a two-minute remark out to ten; when a man's mouth was a rolling-mill, and busied itself all day long in turning four-foot pigs of thought into thirty-foot bars of conversational railroad iron by attenuation; when subjects were seldom faithfully stuck to, but the talk wandered all around and arrived nowhere; when conversations consisted mainly of irrelevancies, with here and there a relevancy, a relevancy with an embarrassed look, as not being able to explain how it got there.

Cooper was certainly not a master in the construction of dialogue. Inaccurate observation defeated him here as it defeated him in so many other enterprises of his. He even failed to notice that the man who talks corrupt English six days in the week must and will talk it on the seventh, and can't help himself. In the *Deerslayer* story he lets *Deerslayer* talk the showiest kind of book-talk sometimes, and at other times the basest of base dialects. For instance, when some one asks him if he has a sweetheart, and if so, where she abides, this is his majestic answer:

"She's in the forest – hanging from the boughs of the trees, in a soft rain – in the dew on the open grass – the clouds that float about in the blue heavens—the birds that sing in the woods – the sweet springs where I slake my thirst – and in all the other glorious gifts that come from God's Providence!"
And he preceded that, a little before, with this:

"It consarns me as all things that touches a fri'nd consarns a fri'nd." …

Cooper's word-sense was singularly dull. When a person has a poor ear for music he will flat and sharp right along without knowing it. He keeps near the tune, but it is not the tune. When a person has a poor ear for words, the result is a literary flatting and sharping; you perceive what he is intending to say, but you also perceive that he doesn't say it. This is Cooper. He was not a word-musician. His ear was satisfied with the approximate word. ...

Now I feel sure, deep down in my heart, that Cooper wrote about the poorest English that exists in our language, and that the English of *Deerslayer* is the very worst that even Cooper ever wrote. ...

I may be mistaken, but it does seem to me that *Deerslayer* is not a work of art in any sense; it does seem to me that it is destitute of every detail that goes to the making of a work of art; in truth, it seems to me that *Deerslayer* is just simply a literary *delirium tremens*.

A work of art? It has no invention; it has no order, system, sequence, or result; it has no life-likeness, no thrill, no stir, no seeming of reality; its characters are confusedly drawn, and by their acts and words they prove that they are not the sort of people the author claims that they are; its humor is pathetic; its pathos is funny; its conversations are – oh! indescribable; its love-scenes odious; its English a crime against the language. Counting these out, what is left is Art. I think we must all admit that.

COPYRIGHT

Whenever a copyright law is to be made or altered, then the idiots assemble.

– *Notebook*, 1902-1903

Only one thing is impossible for God: to find any sense in any copyright law on the planet.

– *Notebook*, 1902-1903

COURAGE

Courage is resistance to fear, mastery of fear – not absence of fear. Except a creature be part coward, it is not a compliment to say he

is brave; it is merely a loose misapplication of the word.
– Pudd'nhead Wilson's Calendar

It is curious – curious that physical courage should be so common in the world, and moral courage so rare.
– Mark Twain in Eruption

COVETOUSNESS

There is no such thing as material covetousness. All covetousness is spiritual. ... Any so-called material thing that you want is merely a symbol: you want it not for itself, but because it will content your spirit for the moment.
– What Is Man?

He had discovered a great law of human action, without knowing it – namely, in order to make a man or a boy covet a thing, it is only necessary to make the thing difficult to attain.
– Adventures of Tom Sawyer

Let us not be too particular. It is better to have old, second-hand diamonds than none at all.
– Following the Equator

COWARDICE

There are several good protections against temptation, but the surest is cowardice.
– Following the Equator

We all live in the protection of certain cowardices which we call our principles.
– More Maxims of Mark, Merle Johnson

The human race is a race of cowards; and I am not only marching in that procession but carrying a banner.
– Mark Twain in Eruption

CRITICISM

A man with a hump-backed uncle mustn't make fun of another man's cross-eyed aunt.
– Mark Twain on England

DEATH

All say, "How hard it is that we have to die" – a strange complaint to come from the mouths of people who have had to live.

> – *The Tragedy of Pudd'nhead Wilson and the Comedy of the Extraordinary Twins*

Death, the refuge, the solace, the best and kindliest and most prized friend and benefactor of the erring, the forsaken, the old and weary and broken of heart.

> – *Adam* speech, 1883

The report of my death was an exaggeration.

> – Letter to the *New York Journal*, June 2, 1897

[Editor's note: Several variations of this quote, and the story that led to it, exist. It's said Twain read his obituary prematurely published in a newspaper (often named as the *New York Journal*) and sent his famous reply in a letter to its editor (or sometimes, in a telegram to The Associated Press). The quote is usually given as, "The report (or reports) of my death are (or have been) greatly exaggerated."]

[God] made a man and a woman and placed them in a pleasant garden, along with the other creatures. They all lived together there in harmony and contentment and blooming youth for some time; then trouble came. God had warned the man and the woman that they must not eat of the fruit of a certain tree. And he added a most strange remark: he said that if they ate of it they should surely die. Strange, for the reason that inasmuch as they had never seen a sample death they could not possibly know what he meant. Neither would he nor any other god have been able to make those ignorant children understand what was meant, without furnishing a sample. The mere word could have no meaning for them, any more than it would have for an infant of days.

> – *Satan's Letter III, Letters from the Earth*

Life was not a valuable gift, but death was. Life was a fever-dream made up of joys embittered by sorrows, pleasure poisoned by pain, a dream that was a nightmare-confusion of spasmodic and fleeting delights, ecstasies, exultations, happinesses, interspersed with long-drawn miseries, griefs, perils, horrors, disappointments, defeats, humiliations, and despairs – the heaviest curse devisable by divine ingenuity; but death was sweet, death was gentle, death was kind; death healed the bruised spirit and the broken heart, and gave them rest and forgetfulness; death was man's best friend; when man could endure life no longer, death came and set him free.

– Satan's Letter X, Letters from the Earth

DECEIT

When a person cannot deceive himself the chances are against his being able to deceive other people.

– Autobiography of Mark Twain

Everyone is a moon, and has a dark side which he never shows to anybody.

– Following the Equator

DEGREES

I take the same childlike delight in a new degree that an Indian takes in a fresh scalp and I take no more pains to conceal my joy than the Indian does.

– Autobiography of Mark Twain

It pleased me beyond measure when Yale made me a Master of Arts, because I didn't know anything about art. ... I rejoiced again when Missouri University made me a Doctor of Laws, because it was all clear profit, I not knowing anything about laws except how to evade them... And now at Oxford I am to be made a Doctor of Letters – all clear profit, because what I don't know about letters would make me a multi-millionaire if I could turn it into cash.

– Autobiography of Mark Twain

DENTISTS

When teeth became touched with decay or were otherwise ailing, the doctor knew of but one thing to do – he fetched his tongs and dragged them out. If the jaw remained, it was not his fault.

– Autobiography of Mark Twain

All dentists talk while they work. They have inherited this from their professional ancestors, the barbers.

– Down the Rhone, Europe and Elsewhere

Some people who can skirt precipices without a tremor have a strong dread of the dentist's chair, whereas I was born without any prejudices against the dentist's chair; when in it I am interested, and not in a hurry, and do not greatly mind the pain. Taken by and large, my style of make has advantages over the other, I think. Few of us are obliged to circumnavigate precipices, but we all have to take a chance at the dental chair.

– Down the Rhone, Europe and Elsewhere

DICTIONARY

I have studied it often, but I never could discover the plot.

– Mark Twain Anecdotes, Cyril Clemens

Oh, that worthless, worthless book, that timid book, that shifty book, that uncertain book, that time-serving book, that exasperating book, that unspeakable book, the Unlimited Dictionary! that book with but one object in life: to get in more and shadings of the words than its competitors. With the result that nearly every time it gets done shading a good old useful word it means everything general and nothing in particular.

– Three Thousand Years Among the Microbes

DIET

In the manner of diet – I have been persistently strict in sticking to the things which didn't agree with me until one or the other of us got the best of it.

– 70th Birthday speech, 1905

DIFFERENCE

It were not best that we should all think alike; it is difference of opinion that makes horse races.

– Pudd'nhead Wilson

People are different. And it is the best way.

– Tom Sawyer, Detective

DILIGENCE

Diligence is a good thing, but taking things easy is much more – restful.

– Speech, March 30, 1901

DINOSAUR

As for the dinosaur – But Noah's conscience was easy; it was not named in his cargo list and he and the boys were not aware that there was such a creature. He said he could not blame himself for not knowing about the dinosaur, because it was an American animal, and America had not then been discovered.

– Adam's Soliloquy

DIPLOMACY

Good breeding consists in concealing how much we think of ourselves and how little we think of the other person.

– Notebook, 1898

I asked Tom if countries always apologized when they had done wrong, and he says – "Yes; the little ones does."

– Tom Sawyer Abroad

DISHONESTY

Yes, even I am dishonest. Not in many ways, but in some. Forty-one, I think it is.

– Letter to Joseph Twichell, March 14, 1905

DOGS

Heaven goes by favor. If it went by merit, you would stay out and your dog would go in.

– Mark Twain, a Biography

If you pick up a starving dog and make him prosperous, he

will not bite you. This is the principal difference between a dog and a man.
— Pudd'nhead Wilson's Calendar

A composite dog is a dog that's made up of all the valuable qualities that's in the dog breed – kind of a syndicate; and a mongrel is made up of the riffraff that's left over.
— Mark Twain in Eruption

The dog is a gentleman; I hope to go to his heaven, not man's.
– Letter to W. D. Howells, April 2, 1899

DOUBT

... our best built certainties are but sand-houses and subject to damage from any wind of doubt that blows.
— The Great Dark

DRINKING

Never refuse to do a kindness unless the act would work great injury to yourself, and never refuse to take a drink – under any circumstances.
— Notebook

I love a drink, but I never encouraged drunkenness by harping on its alleged funny side.
– Quoted in *Abroad with Mark Twain and Eugene Field*, Henry W. Fisher

DUELS

I thoroughly disapprove of duels. I consider them unwise and I know they are dangerous. Also, sinful. If a man should challenge me, I would take him kindly and forgivingly by the hand and lead him to a quiet retired spot and kill him.
— Autobiography of Mark Twain

DUTY

The thing for us to do is our duty. And not to worry about whether anybody sees us or not.
Attrib., 1908

DYING

[Measles] brought me within a shade of death's door. It brought me to where I no longer felt any interest in anything, but, on the contrary, felt a total absence of interest – which was most placid and tranquil and sweet and delightful and enchanting. I have never enjoyed anything in my life any more than I enjoyed dying that time. ... The word had been passed and the family notified to assemble around the bed and see me off. I knew them all. ...They were all crying, but that did not affect me. I took but the vaguest interest in it and that merely because I was the center of all this emotional attention and was gratified by it and vain of it.

– Autobiography of Mark Twain

EDEN

I feel for Adam and Eve now, for I know how it was with them ....The Garden of Eden I now know was an unendurable solitude. I know that the advent of the serpent was a welcome change – anything for society.

– Mark Twain, a Biography

EDITORS

They are conceited and troublesome, and don't pay enough.

– How to Make History Dates Stick, 1899
(first published in *Harper's* magazine, Dec. 1914)

They are full of envy and malice, editors are.

– How to Make History Dates Stick, 1899
(first published in *Harper's* magazine, Dec. 1914)

I am not the editor of a newspaper and shall always try to do right and be good so that God will not make me one.

– Galaxy magazine, 1870

Nobody, except he has tried it, knows what it is to be an editor. It is easy to scribble local rubbish, with the facts all before you; it is easy to clip selections from other papers; it is easy to string out a correspondence from any locality; but it is unspeakable hardship to write editorials.

– Roughing It

How often we recall, with regret, that Napoleon once shot at a magazine editor and missed him and killed a publisher. But we remember with charity, that his intentions were good.
– Letter to Henry Alden, Nov. 11, 1906

I hate editors, for they make me abandon a lot of perfectly good English words.
– Quoted in *Abroad with Mark Twain and Eugene Field*,
Henry W. Fisher

EDUCATION

Training is everything. The peach was once a bitter almond; cauliflower is nothing but cabbage with a college education.
– *Pudd'nhead Wilson's Calendar*

I never let my schooling interfere with my education.
– Attrib.

Everything has its limit – iron ore cannot be educated into gold.
– *What is Man?*

Education consists mainly in what we have unlearned.
– *Notebook*, 1898

ENCHANTMENT

Distance lends enchantment to the view.
– *Mark Twain in Eruption*

EXAMPLE

Few things are harder to put up with than the annoyance of a good example.
– *Pudd'nhead Wilson*

EXPERIENCE

We should be careful to get out of an experience only the wisdom that is in it – and stop there; lest we be like the cat that sits down on a hot stove-lid. She will never sit down on a hot stove-lid again – and that is well; but she will also never sit down on a cold one anymore.

– Following the Equator

Experience teaches us only one thing at a time – and hardly that, in my case.

– Letter to Clara Clemens, Feb. 5, 1893

War talk by men who have been in a war is always interesting; whereas moon talk by a poet who has not been in the moon is likely to be dull.

– Life on the Mississippi

The most permanent lessons in morals are those which come, not of booky teaching, but of experience.

– A Tramp Abroad

FACTS

Get your facts first, and then you can distort them as much as you please.

– Quoted by Rudyard Kipling in *From Sea to Shining Sea*

For a forgotten fact is news when it comes again.

– Following the Equator

FAILURE

It is not in the least likely that any life has ever been lived which was not a failure in the secret judgment of the person who lived it.

– Notebook

FAITH

There are those who scoff at the schoolboy, calling him frivolous and shallow. Yet it was the schoolboy who said, Faith is believing what you know ain't so.

– Following the Equator

FAMILIARITY

Familiarity breeds contempt – and children

– Notebook

FATHER

It is a wise child that knows its own father, and an unusual one that unreservedly approves of him.
– More Maxims of Mark, Merle Johnson, 1927

When I was a boy of fourteen, my father was so ignorant I could hardly stand to have the old man around. But when I got to be twenty-one, I was astonished at how much the old man had learned in seven years.
– Attrib.

FAULT

Always acknowledge a fault frankly. This will throw those in authority off their guard and give you opportunity to commit more.
– More Maxims of Mark, Merle Johnson, 1927

FISHING

Do not tell fish stories where the people know you; but particularly, don't tell them where they know the fish.
– More Maxims of Mark, Merle Johnson, 1927

FLATTERY

Arguments are unsafe with wives, because they examine them; but they do not examine compliments. One can pass upon a wife a compliment that is three-fourths base metal; she will not even bite it to see if it is good; all she notices is the size of it, not the quality.
– Hellfire Hotchkiss

FLIES

Nothing is made in vain, but the fly came near it.
– More Maxims of Mark, Merle Johnson, 1927

FLIRTING

Well, it was touching to see the queen blush and smile, and look embarrassed and happy, and fling furtive glances at Sir

Launcelot that would have got him shot in Arkansas, to a dead certainty.

– A Connecticut Yankee in King Arthur's Court

FOOLS

Let us be thankful for the fools; but for them the rest of us could not succeed.

– Following the Equator

"The trouble isn't that there are too many fools, but that the lightning isn't distributed right."

– Attrib.

If you send a damned fool to St. Louis, and you don't tell them he's a damned fool, they'll never find out.

– Life on the Mississippi

FORBIDDEN

There is a charm about the forbidden that makes it unspeakably desirable.

– Notebook

FORGETFULNESS

I'll forget the Lord's middle name sometime, right in the midst of a storm, when I need all the help I can get.

– Mark Twain, a Biography

FREEDOM

It is by the goodness of God that in our country we have those three unspeakably precious things: freedom of speech, freedom of conscience, and the prudence never to practice either of them.

– Following the Equator

FREE SPEECH

In America – as elsewhere – free speech is confined to the dead.

– Notebook, 1904

FRENCH

In Paris they just simply opened their eyes and stared when we spoke to them in French! We never did succeed in making those idiots understand their own language.

– The Innocents Abroad

The objects of which Paris folks are fond – literature, art, medicine and adultery.

– Corpse speech, 1879

GENIUS

Thousands of geniuses live and die undiscovered – either by themselves or by others.

– Autobiography of Mark Twain

GERMAN

In early times some sufferer had to sit up with a toothache, and he put in the time inventing the German language.

– Notebook #14, 1877-1878

GOD

The gods offer no rewards for intellect. There was never one yet that showed any interest in it...

– Notebook

Man proposes, but God blocks the game.

– Letter to Jean Clemens, June 19, 1908

... being made merely in the image of God, but not otherwise resembling him enough to be mistaken by anybody but a very near-sighted person.

– Letter to sister Pamela, quoted in
The Love Letters of Mark Twain

No man that has ever lived has done a thing to please God –

primarily. It was done to please himself, then God next.

– Mark Twain, a Biography

In God We Trust. I don't believe it would sound any better if it were true.

– Attrib.

We grant God the possession of all the qualities of mind except the one that keeps the others healthy; that watches over their dignity; that focuses their vision true – humor.

– Notebook, 1902

None of us can be as great as God, but any of us can be as good.

– Notebook, 1902-1903

[God] could keep to a bad resolution forever, but he couldn't keep to a good one a month.

– Satan's Letter VI, Letters from the Earth

[Man] concedes that God has made the angels perfect, without blemish, and immune from pain and death, and that he could have been similarly kind to man if he had wanted to, but denies that he was under any moral obligation to do it. He concedes that man has no moral right to visit the child of his begetting with wanton cruelties, painful diseases and death, but refuses to limit God's privileges in this sort with the children of his begetting.

– Satan's Letter VIII, Letters from the Earth

It is claimed that from the beginning of time [God] foresaw everything that would happen in the world. If that is true, he foresaw that Adam and Eve would eat the apple; that their posterity would be unendurable and have to be drowned; that Noah's posterity would in their turn be unendurable, and that by and by he would have to leave his throne in heaven and come down and be crucified to save that same tiresome human race again.

– Satan's Letter IX, Letters from the Earth

It does not appear that [God] ever stopped to reflect that he was to blame when a man went wrong, inasmuch as the man was merely acting in accordance with the disposition he had afflicted him with. No, he punished the man, instead of punishing himself.

– Satan's Letter X, Letters from the Earth

GOODNESS

It is very wearing to be good.

– Life on the Mississippi

GOSSIP

It takes your enemy and your friend, working together to hurt you to the heart; the one to slander you and the other to get the news to you.

– Following the Equator

GREATNESS

Somehow this puissant god seemed to be only a man, after all. How the great do tumble from their high pedestals when we see them in common human flesh, and know that they eat pork and cabbage and act like other men.

– Letter to the San Francisco *Alta California*,
Feb. 5, 1868 (on Charles Dickens)

GRIEF

Nothing that grieves us can be called little: by the eternal laws of proportion a child's loss of a doll and a king's loss of a crown are events of the same size.

– Which Was the Dream?

HABITS

Nothing so needs reforming as other people's habits.

– Pudd'nhead Wilson

HALLEY'S COMET

I came in with Halley's Comet in 1835. It is coming again next year [1910], and I expect to go out with it. It will be the greatest disappointment of my life if I don't go out with Halley's Comet. The Almighty has said, no doubt: "Now here are these two unaccountable freaks; they came in together, they must go out together."
– Mark Twain, a Biography

HAPPINESS

... as happy as a dog with two tails.
– The Adventures of Thomas Jefferson Snodgrass

Sanity and happiness are an impossible combination.
– The Mysterious Stranger

HEALTH

He had had much experience of physicians, and said "the only way to keep your health is to eat what you don't want, drink what you don't like, and do what you'd druther not."
– Following the Equator

Twain's form letter reply to those who recommended medicine:
Dear Sir (or Madam) – I try every remedy sent to me. I am now on No. 67. Yours is 2,653. I am looking forward to its beneficial results.
– Quoted in My Father Mark Twain, Clara Clemens

HEART

It is in the heart that the values lie. I wish I could make him understand that a loving heart is riches, and riches enough, and that without it intellect is poverty.
– Eve's Diary

You can't reason with your heart; it has its own laws, and thumps about things which the intellect scorns.

– *A Connecticut Yankee in King Arthur's Court*

HEAVEN AND HELL

I am silent on the subject because of necessity. I have friends in both places.

– Quoted in *Mark Twain, His Life and Work*, Will Clemens

When I reflect upon the number of disagreeable people who I know have gone to a better world, I am moved to lead a different life.

– *Pudd'nhead Wilson's Calendar*

There is no humor in heaven.

– *Captain Stormfield's Visit to Heaven*

Let us swear while we may, for in Heaven it will not be allowed.

– *Notebook*, 1898

... heaven for climate, and hell for society.

– *Tammany and Croker* speech

His heaven is like himself: strange, interesting, astonishing, grotesque. I give you my word, it has not a single feature in it that he actually values. It consists – utterly and entirely – of diversions which he cares next to nothing about, here in the earth, yet is quite sure he will like them in heaven.

– *Satan's Letter II, Letters from the Earth*

The human being, like the immortals, naturally places sexual intercourse far and away above all other joys – yet he has left it out of his heaven! The very thought of it excites him; opportunity sets him wild; in this state he will risk life, reputation, everything – even his queer heaven itself – to make good that opportunity and ride it to the overwhelming climax. From youth to middle age all men and all women prize copulation above all other pleasures combined, yet it is actually as I have said: it is not in their heaven; prayer takes its place.

– Satan's Letter II, Letters from the Earth

In man's heaven everybody sings! The man who did not sing on earth sings there; the man who could not sing on earth is able to do it there. The universal singing is not casual, not occasional, not relieved by intervals of quiet; it goes on, all day long, and every day, during a stretch of twelve hours. And everybody stays; whereas in the earth the place would be empty in two hours. The singing is of hymns alone. Nay, it is of one hymn alone. The words are always the same, in number they are only about a dozen, there is no rhyme, there is no poetry: "Hosannah, hosannah, hosannah, Lord God of Sabaoth, 'rah! 'rah! 'rah! siss! – boom! ... a-a-ah!"

– Satan's Letter II, Letters from the Earth

All sane white people hate noise; yet they have tranquilly accepted this kind of heaven – without thinking, without reflection, without examination – and they actually want to go to it! Profoundly devout old gray-headed men put in a large part of their time dreaming of the happy day when they will lay down the cares of this life and enter into the joys of that place. Yet you can see how unreal it is to them, and how little it takes a grip upon them as being fact, for they make no practical preparation for the great change: you never see one of them with a harp, you never hear one of them sing.

– Satan's Letter II, Letters from the Earth

HISTORY

History may not repeat itself, but it does rhyme a lot.

Human history in all ages is red with blood, and bitter with hate, and stained with cruelties.

–Satan's Letter XI, Letters from the Earth

HONESTY

Honesty is the best policy – when there is money in it.

– Business speech, March 30, 1901

HONOR

On the whole, it is better to deserve honors and not have them than to have them and not deserve them.

– Notebook, 1902-1903

HUMAN NATURE

There is a great deal of human nature in people.

– Letter to the San Francisco *Alta California*, written May 18, 1867; published June 23, 1867

HUMAN RACE

Such is the human race. Often it does seem such a pity that Noah and his party did not miss the boat.

– Christian Science

There are times when one would like to hang the whole human race, and finish the farce.

– A Connecticut Yankee in King Arthur's Court

Human beings seem to be a poor invention. If they are the noblest works of God where is the ignoblest?

– Notebook, 1896

HUMILITY

There's a breed of humility which is itself a species of showing off.

– The Esquimau Maiden's Romance

HUMOR

Wit and Humor – if any difference it is in – lightning and electric light. Same material, apparently; but one is vivid, brief, and can do damage – the other fools along and enjoys the elaboration.

– Notebook

Against the assault of laughter, nothing can stand.

– The Mysterious Stranger

The funniest things are the forbidden.

– Notebook, 1879

Humor is mankind's greatest blessing.

– Mark Twain, a Biography

IDIOTS

Suppose you were an idiot. And suppose you were a member of Congress. But I repeat myself.

– Mark Twain, a Biography

In the first place God made idiots. This was for practice. Then he made School Boards.

– Following the Equator

The proverb says that Providence protects children and idiots. This is really true. I know because I have tested it.

– Autobiography of Mark Twain

IGNORANCE

The older we grow the greater becomes our wonder at how much ignorance one can contain without bursting one's clothes.

– Mark Twain's Speeches, 1910

I would rather have my ignorance than another man's knowledge, because I have so much more of it.

– Letter to W.D. Howells, Feb. 10, 1875

IMMORTALITY

One of the proofs of the immortality of the soul is that myriads have believed in it. They have also believed the world was flat.

– Notebook, 1900

I have never seen what to me seemed an atom of proof that there is a future life. And yet – I am inclined to expect one.

– Mark Twain, a Biography

INDECISION

I must have a prodigious quantity of mind; it takes me as much as a week sometimes to make it up.

– The Innocents Abroad

INTEGRITY

... it's so hard to find men of a so high type of morals that they'll stay bought.

– Notebook for August 1890-June 1891

INTELLECT

What a fine thing it is to have an intellect, and room enough in the seat of your breeches to hold it.

– marginalia in newspaper article from *The New York Times*, 1908 (reprinted in *Greatness at Your Fingertips*, Bob Slotta)

A man's brain (intellect) is stored powder; it cannot be touched itself off; the fire must come from the outside.

– Notebook, 1898

The gods offer no rewards for intellect. There was never one yet that showed any interest in it...

– Notebook

INVENTORS

Name the greatest of all inventors. Accidents.

– Notebook

A man invents a thing which could revolutionize the arts, produce mountains of money, and bless the earth, and who will bother with it or show any interest in it? –– and so you are just as poor as you were before. But you invent some worthless thing to amuse yourself with, and would throw it away if let alone, and all of a sudden the whole world makes a snatch for it and out crops a fortune.

– The American Claimant

Inventors are the creators of the world – after God.
> – Quoted in *Mark Twain, the Man and His Work*,
> Edward Wagenknecht

I have, as you say, been interested in patents and patentees. If your books tell how to exterminate inventors send me nine editions. Send them by express.
> – *Mark Twain, a Biography*

An inventor is a poet – a true poet – and nothing in any degree less than a high order of poet – wherefore his noblest pleasure dies with the stroke that completes the creature of his genius, just as the painter's & the sculptor's & other poets' highest pleasure ceases with the touch that finishes their work – & so only he can understand or appreciate the legitimate "success" of his achievement, little minds being able to get no higher than a comprehension of a vulgar moneyed success.
> – Letter to Pamela Moffett, June 12, 1870

Every great invention takes a livelihood away from 50,000 men – & within ten years creates a livelihood for half a million. But you can't make Labor appreciate that: he is laboring for himself, not the breadless half million that are issuing from his loins. They are somebody else's children; he fails to reflect that his own are among them.
> – Letter to W. D. Howells, March 31, 1888

INVITATIONS

It is easier to decline 20 invitations than to accept one & then explain to the other nineteen.
> – Letter to William Ellsworth, 1902

IRREVERENCE

True irreverence is disrespect for another man's god.
> – *Following the Equator*

Irreverence is another person's disrespect to your god; there isn't any word that tells what your disrespect to his god is.
> – *The Mysterious Stranger*

When a thing is sacred to me it is impossible for me to be irreverent toward it. I cannot call to mind a single instance where I have ever been irreverent, except toward the things which were sacred to other people.

– Is Shakespeare Dead?

Irreverence is the champion of liberty and its only sure defense.

– Notebook, 1888

ITALIANS

We have the notion in our country that Italians never do heavy work at all, but confine themselves to the lighter arts, like organ-grinding, operatic singing, and assassination. We have blundered, that is plain.

– A Tramp Abroad

They examine passports on the Italian frontier for fear an honest man may slip in.

– Notebook #16, August-October 1878

ITCH

If you are with the quality, or at a funeral, or trying to go to sleep when you ain't sleepy – if you are anywheres where it won't do for you to scratch, why you will itch all over in upward of a thousand places.

– Adventures of Huckleberry Finn

JACKASS

Concerning the difference between man and the jackass: some observers hold that there isn't any. But this wrongs the jackass.

– Notebook, 1898

There is no character, howsoever good and fine, but it can be destroyed by ridicule, howsoever poor and witless. Observe the ass, for instance: his character is about perfect, he is the choicest spirit among all the humbler animals, yet see what ridicule has brought him to. Instead of feeling complimented when we are called an ass, we are left in doubt.

– Pudd'nhead Wilson

JAILS

Every time you stop a school, you will have to build a jail. What you gain at one end you lose at the other. It's like feeding a dog on his own tail. It won't fatten the dog.

– Speech, Nov. 23, 1900

JEALOUSY

Among human beings jealousy ranks distinctly as a weakness; a trademark of small minds; a property of all small minds, yet a property which even the smallest is ashamed of; and when accused of its possession will lyingly deny it and resent the accusation as an insult.

– Satan's Letter VI, Letters from the Earth

JESUS

Jesus died to save men – a small thing for an immortal to do, & didn't save many, anyway; but if he had been damned for the race that would have been an act of a size proper to a god, & would have saved the whole race. However, why should anybody want to save the human race, or damn it either? Does God want its society? Does Satan?

– Notebook #42

The two Testaments are interesting, each in its own way. The Old one gives us a picture of these people's Deity as he was before he got religion, the other one gives us a picture of him as he appeared afterward. The Old Testament is interested mainly in blood and sensuality. The New one in Salvation. Salvation by fire. The first time the Deity came down to earth, he brought life and death; when he came the second time, he brought hell.

– Satan's Letter X, Letters from the Earth

JEWS

For I am without prejudice. It is my hope that both the Christians and the Jews will be damned; and to that end I am working all my influence. Help me pray... If I have any leaning it is toward the Jew, not the Christian. (There is one thing I'd like to say, but I dasn't: Christianity has deluged the world with blood and tears – Judaism has caused neither for religion's sake.)

– Letter to Henry Huddleston Rogers

It's a marvelous race – by long odds the most marvelous that the world has produced, I suppose.

– Letter to Joseph Twichell, Oct. 23, 1897

The Jews have the best average brain of any people in the world. The Jews are the only race who work wholly with their brains and never with their hands... They are peculiarly and conspicuously the world's intellectual aristocracy.

– *Notebook*

Even if the Jews have not all been geniuses, their general average of intelligence and intellectuality is far above our general average – and that is one of our reasons for wishing to drive them out of the higher forms of business and the professions. It is the swollen envy of pigmy minds – meanness, injustice.

– Quoted in *My Husband Gabrilowitsch*, Clara Clemens

JOURNAL

If you wish to inflict a heartless and malignant punishment upon a young person, pledge him to keep a journal a year.

– *The Innocents Abroad*

JOURNALISM

Journalism is the one solitary respectable profession which honors theft (when committed in the pecuniary interest of a journal,) & admires the thief... However, these same journals combat despicable crimes quite valiantly – when committed in other quarters.

– Letter to W. D. Howells, Oct. 30, 1880

I am personally acquainted with hundreds of journalists, and the opinion of the majority of them would not be worth tuppence in private, but when they speak in print it is the newspaper that is talking (the pygmy scribe is not visible) and then their utterances shake the community like the thunders of prophecy.

– Speech, 1873

JOY

Grief can take care of itself, but to get full value of a joy you must have somebody to divide it with.

– Following the Equator

JUDGMENT

I'd rather have a sound judgment than a talent.

– The American Vandal Abroad speech

You cannot depend on your judgment when your imagination is out of focus.

– Notebook

JURY

We have a criminal jury system which is superior to any in the world; and its efficiency is only marred by the difficulty of finding twelve men every day who don't know anything and can't read.

– Fourth of July speech, 1873

The jury system puts a ban upon intelligence and honesty, and a premium upon ignorance, stupidity and perjury. It is a shame that we must continue to use a worthless system because it was good a thousand years ago.

– Roughing It

JUSTICE

The rain ...falls upon the just and the unjust alike; a thing which would not happen if I were superintending the rain's affairs. No, I would rain softly and sweetly on the just, but if I caught a sample of the unjust outdoors I would drown him.

– Mark Twain, a Biography

KALEIDOSCOPE

I don't see why a kaleidoscope shouldn't enjoy itself as much as a telescope nor a grindstone have as good a time as a whetstone, nor a barometer as good a time as a yardstick.

– Unsent letter to Orion Clemens, Feb. 9, 1879

KELLER, HELEN

I am filled with the wonder of her knowledge, acquired because shut out from all distractions. If I could have been deaf, dumb, and blind I also might have arrived at something.

– Mark Twain's Speeches

KILLING

If the desire to kill and the opportunity to kill came always together, who would escape hanging?

– Following the Equator

KINDNESS

Never refuse to do a kindness unless the act would work great injury to yourself, and never refuse to take a drink – under any circumstances.

– Notebook

KINGS

... there is nothing diviner about a king than there is about a tramp, after all. He is just a cheap and hollow artificiality when you don't know he is a king. But reveal his quality, and dear me, it takes your breath away to look at him. I reckon we are all fools. Born so, no doubt.

– A Connecticut Yankee in King Arthur's Court

Kings is mostly rapscallions.

– Adventures of Huckleberry Finn

Monarchs are usurpers and descendants of usurpers; for the reason that no throne was ever set up in this world by the will, freely exercised, of the only body possessing the legitimate right to set it up – the numerical mass of the nation.

– Letter to Sylvester Baxter, 1889

KIPLING, RUDYARD

He is a stranger to me, but he is a most remarkable man – and I am the other one. Between us, we cover all knowledge; he knows all that can be known, and I know the rest.

– Mark Twain in Eruption

Since England and America have been joined in Kipling, may they not be severed in Twain.

– Authors Club speech, London, 1899

KNOWLEDGE

All schools, all colleges, have two great functions: to confer, and to conceal, valuable knowledge. The theological knowledge which they conceal cannot justly be regarded as less valuable than that which they reveal. That is, when a man is buying a basket of strawberries it can profit him to know that the bottom half of it is rotten.

– Notebook 1908

For all the talk you hear about knowledge being such a wonderful thing, instinct is worth forty of it for real unerringness.

– Tom Sawyer Abroad

We have not the reverent feeling for the rainbow that the savage has, because we know how it is made. We have lost as much as we gained by prying into that matter.

– A Tramp Abroad

Sir, I have been through it from Alpha to Omaha, and I tell you that the less a man knows the bigger the noise he makes and the higher the salary he commands.

– How I Edited an Agricultural Paper, 1870

You may have noticed that the less I know about a subject the more confidence I have, and the more new light I throw on it.

– A Bibliography of Mark Twain, Merle Johnson, 1935

I was gratified to be able to answer promptly and I did. I said I didn't know.

– Life on the Mississippi

But we are all that way: when we know a thing we have only scorn for other people who don't happen to know it.

– Personal Recollections of Joan of Arc

Supposing is good, but finding out is better.

– Mark Twain in Eruption

LANGUAGE

But language is a treacherous thing, a most unsure vehicle, and it can seldom arrange descriptive words in such a way that they will not inflate the facts –by help of the reader's imagination, which is always ready to take a hand and work for nothing, and do the bulk of it at that.

– Following the Equator

LAUGHTER

Will a day come when the race will detect the funniness of these juvenilities and laugh at them – and by laughing at them destroy them? For your race, in its poverty, has unquestionably one really effective weapon – laughter. Power, Money, Persuasion, Supplication, Persecution – these can lift at a colossal humbug – push it a little – crowd it a little – weaken it a little, century by century: but only Laughter can blow it to rags and atoms at a blast. Against the assault of Laughter nothing can stand.

– The Chronicle of Young Satan, Mysterious Stranger manuscripts

He laughs best who laughs least.
> – Autographed inscription to Louisa Payne, Feb. 3, 1909

LAUNDRY

German laundry could not have acquired this perfect igno-rance of how to do up a shirt without able instruction – one easily sees England in it. Your collar is like a horse-collar; your shirt can stand alone and when you get into it you feel ready for crime. It is a wonder they do not have more crime here, but it is increasing as adoption of clean shirts spreads among the social democrats.
> – *Notebook*

LAW

Those people ... early stricken of God, intellectually – the de-partmental interpreters of the laws in Washington ... can al-ways be depended on to take any reasonably good law and interpret the common sense all out of it.
> – Unmailed letter to H. C. Christiancy, Dec. 18, 1887

If we only had some God in the country's laws, instead of be-ing in such a sweat to get him into the Constitution, it would be better all around.
> – Letter to W. D. Howells, Sept. 18, 1875

The laws of Nature, that is to say the laws of God, plainly made every human being a law unto himself, we must steadfastly refuse to obey those laws, and we must as steadfastly stand by the conventions which ignore them, since the statutes furnish us peace, fairly good government, and stability, and therefore are better for us than the laws of God, which would soon plunge us into confusion and disorder and anarchy if we should adopt them.
> – *Mark Twain in Eruption*

We have an insanity plea that would have saved Cain.
> – *Fourth of July* speech, 1873

It would not be possible for Noah to do in our day what he was permitted to do in his own... The inspector would come and examine the Ark, and make all sorts of objections.

– About All Kinds of Ships, 1892

LAWYERS

Lawyers are like other people – fools on the average; but it is easier for an ass to succeed in that trade than any other.

– Quoted in *Sam Clemens of Hannibal*, Dixon Wecter

LAZINESS

I am no lazier now than I was forty years ago, but that is because I reached the limit forty years ago. You can't go beyond possibility.

– Mark Twain in Eruption

LETTERS

When you get an exasperating letter what happens? If you are young, you answer it promptly, instantly – and mail the thing you have written. At forty what do you do? By that time you have found out that a letter written in passion is a mistake in ninety-nine cases out of a hundred.

– Mark Twain, a Biography

An old, cold letter …makes you wonder how you could ever have got into such a rage about nothing.

– Mark Twain, a Biography

The reason I dread writing letters is because I am so apt to get to slinging wisdom & forget to let up. Thus much precious time is lost.

– Letter to James Redpath, June 15, 1871

Now in pleasanter days, I had amused myself with writing letters to the chief paper of the Territory, the Virginia daily *Territorial Enterprise*, and had always been surprised when they appeared in print. My good opinion of its editors had steadily declined; for it seemed to me that they might have found something better to fill up with than my literature.

– Roughing it

LIBERTY

Irreverence is the champion of liberty.

– Notebook, 1888

LIES

You cain't pray a lie.

– Adventures of Huckleberry Finn

Carlyle said "a lie cannot live." It shows that he did not know how to tell them.

– Mark Twain's Autobiography; Mark Twain in Eruption

The most outrageous lies that can be invented will find believers if a man only tells them with all his might.

– Letter to San Francisco *Alta California*, dated May 17, 1867; published June 16, 1867

[Lying is] Man's most universal weakness.

– Quoted in *Mark Twain and I*, Opie Read

LIFE

Human life is maliciously planned with one principal object in view:to make you do all the different kinds of things you particularly don't want to do.

– Notes added in April, 1909 to a letter to W. D. Howells, Nov. 17, 1878

LIGHTNING

Thunder is good, thunder is impressive; but it is lightning that does the work.

– Letter, Aug. 28, 1908

LIQUOR

Taking the pledge will not make bad liquor into good, but it will improve it.

– More Maxims of Mark, Merle Johnson, 1927

How I do hate those enemies of the human race who go around enslaving God's free people with pledges – to quit drinking instead of to quit wanting to drink.

– Letter to Henry W. Beecher, Sept. 11, 1885

LONESOME

Be good and you will be lonesome.

– Frontispiece from first edition of Following the Equator

LOTTERY

The lottery is a government institution & the poor its best patrons.

– Notebook #17, October 1878-February 1879

LOVE

When you fish for love, bait with your heart, not your brain.

– Notebook, 1898

Love seems the swiftest, but it is the slowest of all growths. No man or woman really knows what perfect love is until they have been married a quarter of a century.

– Notebook

Love is not a product of reasonings and statistics. It just comes – none knows whence – and cannot explain itself.

– Eve's Diary

Love is a madness; if thwarted it develops fast.

– The Memorable Assassination

The frankest and freest product of the human mind and heart is a love letter; the writer gets his limitless freedom of statement and expression from his sense that no stranger is going to see what he is writing.

– Mark Twain's Autobiography, 1959 (preface)

True love is the only heart disease that is best left to "run on" – the only affliction of the heart for which there is no help, and none desired.

– Notebook

The course of free love never runs smooth. I suppose we have all tried it.

– Notebook, 1904

LOYALTY

The first thing I want to teach is disloyalty till they get used to disusing that word loyalty as representing a virtue. This will beget independence – which is loyalty to one's best self and principles, and this is often disloyalty to the general idols and fetishes.

– Notebook

Loyalty to petrified opinion never yet broke a chain or freed a human soul in this world – and never will.

– Consistency speech

LUCK

A dollar picked up in the road is more satisfaction to you than the ninety-and -nine which you had to work for, and money won at faro or in stock snuggles into your heart in the same way.

– The Shrine of St. Wagner

MADNESS

Of course, no man is entirely in his right mind at any time.

– The Mysterious Stranger

... in one way or another all men are mad. Many are mad for money... Love is a madness ... it can grow to a frenzy of despair ... All the whole list of desires, predilections, aversions, ambitions, passions, cares, griefs, regrets, remorses, are incipient madness, and ready to grow, spread and consume, when the occasion comes. There are no healthy minds, and nothing saves any man but accident – the accident of not having his malady put to the supreme test. One of the commonest forms of madness is the desire to be noticed, the pleasure derived from being noticed. Perhaps it is not merely common, but universal.

– The Memorable Assassination

When we remember we are all mad, the mysteries of life disappear and life stands explained.

– Notebook, 1898

MAJORITY

Whenever you find yourself on the side of the majority, it is time to reform (or pause and reflect).

– Notebook, 1904

MALICE

Of all the creatures [man] ... is the only one – the solitary one – that possesses malice. ... He is the only creature that inflicts pain for sport, knowing it to be pain ... all creatures kill ... man is the only one ... that kills in malice, the only one that kills for revenge.

– Mark Twain's Autobiography

Malice and malignity faded out of me – or maybe I drove them out of me, knowing that a malignant book would hurt nobody but the fool who wrote it.

– Letter to W. D. Howells, Jan. 28, 1882

There is more real pleasure to be gotten out of a malicious act, where your heart is in it, than out of thirty acts of a nobler sort.

– Mark Twain in Eruption

MAN

Man is the only animal that blushes. Or needs to.
– Following the Equator

Of all the animals, man is the only one that is cruel. He is the only one that inflicts pain for the pleasure of doing it.
– The Lowest Animal

Man was made at the end of the week's work when God was tired.
– Notebook

I believe our Heavenly Father invented man because he was disappointed in the monkey.
– Mark Twain in Eruption

Man is an experiment, the other animals are another experiment. Time will show whether they were worth the trouble.
– God to Satan, Letters from the Earth

This is a strange place, and extraordinary place, and interesting. There is nothing resembling it at home. The people are all insane, the other animals are all insane, the earth is insane, Nature itself is insane. Man is a marvelous curiosity. When he is at his very, very best he is a sort of low-grade nickel-plated angel; at his worst he is unspeakable, unimaginable; and first and last and all the time he is a sarcasm. Yet he blandly and in all sincerity calls himself the "noblest work of God."
– Satan's Letter I, Letters from the Earth

[Man] thinks he is the Creator's pet. He believes the Creator is proud of him; he even believes the Creator loves him; has a passion for him; sits up nights to admire him; yes, and watch over him and keep him out of trouble. He prays to Him, and thinks He listens.
– Satan's Letter I, Letters from the Earth

Man is without any doubt the most interesting fool there is.
– Satan's Letter VIII, Letters from the Earth

MARRIAGE

Separately, foreign marriages and whisky are bad; mixed, they are fatal.

– Letter to Olivia Clemens, June 3, 1895

Men and women – even man and wife are foreigners. Each has reserves that the other cannot enter into, nor understand. These have the effect of frontiers.

– *Notebook, 1904*

What a world of trouble those who never marry escape! There are many happy matches, it is true, and sometimes "my dear," and my love" come from the heart; but what sensible bachelor, rejoicing in his freedom and years of discretion, will run the tremendous risk?

– *Connubial Bliss, Hannibal Journal*, Nov. 4, 1852

Marriage – yes, it is the supreme felicity of life. I concede it. And it is also the supreme tragedy of life. The deeper the love the surer the tragedy. And the more disconsolating when it comes.

– Letter to Father Fitz-Simon, June 5, 1908

Both marriage and death ought to be welcome: the one promises happiness, doubtless the other assures it.

– Letter to Will Bowen, Nov. 4, 1888

People talk about beautiful friendships between two persons of the same sex. What is the best of that sort, as compared with the friendship of man and wife, where the best impulses and highest ideals of both are the same. There is no place for comparison between the two friendships; the one is earthly, the other divine.

– *A Connecticut Yankee in King Arthur's Court*

If husbands could realize what large returns of profit may be gotten out of a wife by a small word of praise paid over the counter when the market is just right, they would bring matters around the way they wish them much oftener than they usually do. Arguments are unsafe with wives, because they examine them; but they do not examine compliments. One can pass upon a wife a compliment that is three-fourths base metal; she will not even bite it to see if it is good; all she notices is the size of it, not the quality.

– Hellfire Hotchkiss

There isn't time – so brief is life – for bickerings, apologies, heartburnings, callings to account. There is only time for loving – & but an instant, so to speak, for that.

– Letter to Clara Spaulding, Aug. 20, 1886

MARTYRDOM

Martyrdom covers a multitude of sins.

– Notebook, 1902-1903

Martyrdom is the luckiest fate that can befall some people.

– A Tramp Abroad

MAXIM

What are the proper proportions of a maxim? A minimum of sound to a maximum of sense.

– Holograph, Dec. 12, 1897

It is more trouble to make a maxim than it is to do right.

– Following the Equator

MEMORY

When I was younger, I could remember anything, whether it had happened or not; but my faculties are decaying now and soon I shall be so I cannot remember any but the things that never happened.

– Autobiography of Mark Twain

It isn't so astonishing, the number of things that I can remember, as the number of things I can remember that aren't so.

– Mark Twain, a Biography

MERIT

Merit alone should constitute the one title to eminence, and we Americans can afford to look down and spit upon miserable titled nonentities.

– Interview, Dec. 1889

I am prouder to have climbed up to where I am just by sheer natural merit than I would be to ride the very sun in the zenith and have to reflect that I was nothing but a poor little accident, and got shot up there out of somebody else's catapult. To me, merit is everything – in fact, the only thing. All else is dross.

– Personal Recollections of Joan of Arc

MILK

I prefer milk because I am a Prohibitionist, but I do not go to it for inspiration.

– Queen Victoria's Jubilee

MIND

I have a prodigious quantity of mind; it takes me as much as a week sometimes to make it up.

– The Innocents Abroad

MIRACLE

There is nothing more awe-inspiring than a miracle except the credulity that can take it at par.

– Notebook, 1904

The difference between a Miracle and a Fact is exactly the difference between a mermaid and seal. It could not be expressed better.

– Letters From the Earth

MISFORTUNE

Nothing that grieves us can be called little: by the eternal laws of proportion a child's loss of a doll and a king's loss of a crown are events of the same size.

– Which Was the Dream?

... the size of a misfortune is not determinable by an outsider's measurement of it, but only by the measurement applied to it by the person specially affected by it. The king's lost crown is a vast matter to the king, but of no consequence to the child. The lost toy is a great matter to the child, but in the king's eyes it is not a thing to break the heart about.

– Autobiography of Mark Twain

MISSIONARIES

We are all missionaries (propagandists of our views.) Each of us disapproves of the other missionaries.

– Notebook, 1905

MISSISSIPPI RIVER

The Mississippi River will always have its own way; no engineering skill can persuade it to do otherwise...

– Mark Twain in Eruption

In the space of one hundred and seventy-six years the Lower Mississippi has shortened itself two hundred and forty-two miles. That is an average of a trifle over one mile and a third per year. Therefore, any calm person, who is not blind or idiotic, can see that in the Old Oolitic Silurian Period, just a million years ago next November, the Lower Mississippi River was upwards of one million three hundred thousand miles long, and stuck out over the Gulf of Mexico like a fishing-rod. And by the same token any person can see that seven hundred and forty-two years from now the Lower Mississippi will be only a mile and three-quarters long, and Cairo and New Orleans will have joined their streets together, and be plodding comfortably along under a single mayor and a mutual board of aldermen. There is something fascinating about science. One gets such wholesale returns of conjecture out of such a trifling investment of fact.

– Life on the Mississippi

MOB

The pitifulest thing out is a mob; that's what an army is – a mob; they don't fight with courage that's born in them, but with courage that's borrowed from their mass, and from their officers. But a mob without any man at the head of it, is beneath pitifulness.
– Adventures of Huckleberry Finn

MODERN

… all the modern inconveniences.
– Letter to J. Y. M. MacAlister, Sept. 1900;
also in *Life on the Mississippi*

MODESTY

Modesty antedates clothes and will be resumed when clothes are no more. Modesty died when clothes were born. Modesty died when false modesty was born.
– Mark Twain, a Biography

The man who is ostentatious of his modesty is twin to the statue that wears a fig leaf.
– Following the Equator

I was born modest; not all over, but in spots.
– A Connecticut Yankee in King Arthur's Court

MONA LISA

To me it was merely a serene and subdued face, and there an end. There might be more in it, but I could not find it. The complexion was bad; in fact, it was not even human; there are no people that color.
– Down the Rhone, Europe and Elsewhere

MONARCHY

There are shams and shams; there are frauds and frauds, but the transparentest of all is the sceptered one. We see monarchs meet and go through solemn ceremonies, farces, with straight countenances; but it is not possible to imagine them meeting in private and not laughing in each other's faces.

– Notebook

I wish I might live fifty years longer; I believe I should see the thrones of Europe selling at auction for old iron. I believe I should really see the end of what is surely the grotesquest of all the swindles ever invented by man – monarchy.

– Letter to Sylvester Baxter of the *Boston Herald*, 1889

MONEY

The lack of money is the root of all evil.

– More Maxims of Mark, Merle Johnson, 1927

Some men worship rank, some worship heroes, some worship power, some worship God, & over these ideals they dispute & cannot unite – but they all worship money.

– Notebook

MORALITY

There is Moral Sense, and there is an Immoral Sense. History shows us that the Moral Sense enables us to perceive morality and how to avoid it, and that the Immoral Sense enables us to perceive immorality and how to enjoy it.

– Following the Equator

The Moral Sense teaches us what is right, and how to avoid it – when unpopular.

– The United States of Lyncherdom

Whenever I look at the other animals and realize that whatever they do is blameless and they can't do wrong, I envy them the dignity of their estate, its purity and its loftiness, and recognize that the Moral Sense is a thoroughly disastrous thing.

– What Is Man?

The low level which commercial morality has reached in America is deplorable. We have humble God-fearing Christian men among us who will stoop to do things for a million dollars that they ought not to be willing to do for less than 2 millions.

– *Notebook, 1902*

It is curious that physical courage should be so common in the world, and moral courage so rare.

– *Mark Twain in Eruption*

It's my opinion that every one I know has morals, though I wouldn't like to ask. I know I have. But I'd rather teach them than practice them any day. "Give them to others" – that's my motto.

– *Morals and Memory* speech

Morals consist of political morals, commercial morals, ecclesiastical morals, and morals.

– *More Maxims of Mark*, Merle Johnson, 1927

We get our morals from books. I didn't get mine from books, but I know that morals do come from books – theoretically, at least.

– Remarks at the opening of the Mark Twain Library

A man should not be without morals; it is better to have bad morals than none at all.

– *Notebook*

Morals are an acquirement – like music, like a foreign language, like piety, poker, paralysis – no man is born with them.

– Quoted in a *Mark Twain Calendar*, March 1917

MORMONS

"All men have heard of the Mormon Bible, but few except the "elect" have seen it, or, at least, taken the trouble to read it. I brought away a copy from Salt Lake. The book is a curiosity to me, it is such a pretentious affair, and yet so "slow," so sleepy, such an insipid mess of inspiration. It is chloroform in print. If Joseph Smith composed this book, the act was a miracle – keeping awake while he did it was, at any rate. If he, according to tradition, merely translated it from certain ancient and mysteriously engraved plates of copper, which he declares he found under a stone in an out-of-the-way locality, the work of translating was equally a miracle, for the same reason.

The book seems to be merely a prosy detail of imaginary history, with the Old Testament for a model; followed by a tedious plagiarism of the New Testament. The author labored to give his words and phrases the quaint, old-fashioned sound and structure of our King James' translation of the Scriptures; and the result is a mongrel-half modern glibness, and half ancient simplicity and gravity. The latter is awkward and constrained; the former natural, but grotesque by the contrast. Whenever he found his speech growing too modern – which was about every sentence or two – he ladled in a few such scriptural phrases as "exceeding sore," "and it came to pass," etc., and made things satisfactory again. "And it came to pass" was his pet. If he had left that out, his Bible would have been only a pamphlet.

...The Mormon Bible is rather stupid and tiresome to read, but there is nothing vicious in its teachings. Its code of morals is unobjectionable – it is "smouched" from the New Testament and no credit given.

– Roughing It

Am I a friend to the Mormon religion? No. I would like to see it extirpated, but always by fair means, not these Congressional rascalities. If you can destroy it with a book, – by arguments and facts, not brute force – you will do a good and wholesome work.

– Letter to Miss Kate Field, March 8, 1886

MUSIC

All of us contain Music & Truth, but most of us can't get it out.
– autograph for Stefan Czapka, quoted in *Our Famous Guest: Mark Twain in Vienna*, Carl Dolmetsch

We often feel sad in the presence of music without words; and often more than that in the presence of music without music.
– *More Maxims of Mark*, Merle Johnson, 1927

NAMES

... it must be intensely annoying to the spirit of a defunct warrior to know that, after having laid down his life for fame, his name has been misspelt in the papers.
– Letter of Quintus Curtius Snodgrass, reprinted in *The Twainian*, July, 1942

... when a teacher calls a boy by his entire name it means trouble.
– *Mark Twain in Eruption*

NATION

A nation is only an individual multiplied.
– *The Turning-Point of My Life*

NATURE

Nature knows no indecencies; man invents them.
– *Notebook*

Nature makes the locust with an appetite for crops; man would have made him with an appetite for sand – I mean a man with the least little bit of common sense.
– *Following the Equator*

NECESSITY

Necessity is the mother of taking chances.
– *Roughing It*

Necessity knows no law.
– *The Innocents Abroad*

All men know that few things that are done from necessity have much fascination about them.
– Letter to Olivia Clemens, Jan. 24, 1869

NEGROES

In the case of the Negro it is of course very different. The majority of us do not like his features, or his color, and we forget to notice that his heart is often a damned sight better than ours.
– Quoted in *My Husband Gabrilowitsch*, Clara Clemens

I do not believe I would very cheerfully help a white student who would ask a benevolence of a stranger, but I do not feel so about the other color. We have ground the manhood out of them, & the shame is ours, not theirs, & we should pay for it.
– Letter to Francis Wayland, Dec. 24, 1885

NEVADA

Some people are malicious enough to think that if the devil were set at liberty and told to confine himself to Nevada Territory, he would ... get homesick and go back to hell again.
– *Mark Twain, a Biography*

[In early Nevada] there was but little realty to tax, and it did seem as if nobody was ever going to think of the simple salvation of inflicting a money penalty on murder.
– *Roughing It*

NEW ORLEANS

But the people cannot have wells, and so they take rain-water. Neither can they conveniently have cellars or graves, the town being built upon "made ground"; so they do without both, and few of the living complain, and none of the others.
– *Life on the Mississippi*

NEW YEAR'S EVE

Now is the accepted time to make your regular annual good resolutions. Next week you can begin paving hell with them as usual. Yesterday, everybody smoked his last cigar, took his last drink, and swore his last oath. Today, we are a pious and exemplary community. Thirty days from now, we shall have cast our reformation to the winds and gone to cutting our ancient shortcomings considerably shorter than ever. We shall also reflect pleasantly upon how we did the same old thing last year about this time. However, go in, community. New Year's is a harmless annual institution of no particular use to anybody save as a scapegoat for promiscuous drunks, and friendly calls, and humbug resolutions, and we wish you to enjoy it with a looseness suited to the greatness of the occasion.

– Editorial in *The Territorial Enterprise*,
Virginia City, Nevada, 1862

NEW YORK

All men in New York insult you – there seem to be no exceptions. There are exceptions of course – have been – but they are probably dead. I am speaking of all persons there who are clothed in a little brief authority.

– *Notebook #24*, April-Aug. 1885

There is one thing very sure – I can't keep my temper in New York. The cars and carriages always come along and get in the way just as I want to cross a street, and if there is any thing that can make a man soar into flights of sublimity in the matter of profanity, it is that thing.

– Letter to San Francisco *Alta California*, June 5, 1867

You do not swear anymore now, of course, because you can't find any words that are long enough or strong enough to fit the case. You feel degraded and ignominious and subjugated. And there and then you say that you will go away from New York and start over again; and that you will never come back to settle permanently till you have learned to swear with the utmost fluency in seventeen different languages.

– Letter to San Francisco *Alta California*, June 5, 1867

I have at last, after several months' experience, made up my mind that it is a splendid desert – a domed and steepled solitude, where the stranger is lonely in the midst of a million of his race. A man walks his tedious miles through the same interminable street every day, elbowing his way through a buzzing multitude of men, yet never seeing a familiar face, and never seeing a strange one the second time. He visits a friend once – it is a day's journey – and then stays away from that time forward till that friends cools to a mere acquaintance, and finally to a stranger. So there is little sociability, and consequently, there is little cordiality. Every man seems to feel that he has got the duties of two lifetimes to accomplish in one, and so he rushes, rushes, rushes, and never has time to be companionable – never has any time at his disposal to fool away on matters which do not involve dollars and duty and business.

– Letter to San Francisco *Alta California*, June 5, 1867

There is something about this ceaseless buzz, and hurry, and bustle, that keeps a stranger in a state of unwholesome excitement all the time, and makes him restless and uneasy, and saps from him all capacity to enjoy anything or take a strong interest in any matter whatever – a something which impels him to try to do everything, and yet permits him to do nothing. He is a boy in a candy-shop – could choose quickly if there were but one kind of candy, but is hopelessly undetermined in the midst of a hundred kinds. A stranger feels unsatisfied, here, a good part of the time.

– Letter to San Francisco *Alta California*, June 5, 1867

NEWPORT, RHODE ISLAND

Newport, Rhode Island, that breeding place – that stud farm, so to speak – of aristocracy; aristocracy of the American type.

– *Autobiography of Mark Twain*

NEWSPAPERS

Our newspapers are abused. We are told that they are irreverent, coarse, vulgar, ribald. I hope they will remain irreverent. I would like that irreverence to be preserved in America forever and ever – irreverence for all royalties and all those titled creatures born into privilege.

– Interview, Dec., 1889

We like to read about rich people in the newspapers; the papers know it, and they do their best to keep this appetite liberally fed.

– Mark Twain in Eruption

There is no suffering comparable with that which a private person feels when he is for the first time pilloried in print.

– Life on the Mississippi

The old saw says, "Let sleeping dogs lie." Right. Still when there is much at stake it is better to get a newspaper to do it.

– Following the Equator

... one of the worst things about civilization is, that anybody that gits a letter with trouble in it comes and tells you all about it and makes you feel bad, and the newspapers fetches you the troubles of everybody all over the world, and keeps you downhearted and dismal most all the time, and it's such a heavy load for a person.

– Tom Sawyer Abroad

... news is history in its first and best form, its vivid and fascinating form, and ... history is the pale and tranquil reflection of it.

– Autobiography of Mark Twain

It seems to me that just in the ratio that our newspapers increase, our morals decay. The more newspapers the worse morals. Where we have one newspaper that does good, I think we have fifty that do harm. We ought to look upon the establishment of a newspaper of the average pattern in a virtuous village as a calamity.

– License of the Press speech

It has become a sarcastic proverb that a thing must be true if you saw it in a newspaper. That is the opinion intelligent people have of that lying vehicle in a nutshell. But the trouble is that the stupid people – who constitute the grand overwhelming majority of this and all other nations – do believe and are moulded and convinced by what they get out of a newspaper, and there is where the harm lies.

– License of the Press speech

Our papers have one peculiarity – it is American – their irreverence... They are irreverent toward pretty much everything, but where they laugh one good king to death, they laugh a thousand cruel and infamous shams and superstitions into the grave, and the account is squared. Irreverence is the champion of liberty and its only sure defense.

– Notebook

NIAGARA FALLS

You can descend a staircase here a hundred and fifty feet down, and stand at the edge of the water. After you have done it, you will wonder why you did it; but you will then be too late.

– Niagara, Sketches Old and New

There is no actual harm in making Niagara a background whereon to display one's marvelous insignificance in a good strong light, but it requires a sort of superhuman self-complacency to enable one to do it.

– Niagara, Sketches Old and New

NIGHT

In my age, as in my youth, night brings me many a deep remorse. I realize that from the cradle up I have been like the rest of the race – never quite sane in the night.

– Autobiography of Mark Twain

NOBLE

To be good is noble, but to teach others how to be good is nobler – and less trouble.

– Doctor Van Dyke speech, 1906

NOBILITY

A monarch when good is entitled to the consideration which we accord to a pirate who keeps Sunday School between crimes; when bad he is entitled to none at all. But if you cross a king with a prostitute the resulting mongrel perfectly satisfies the English idea of nobility.

– Notebook

Essentially, nobilities are foolishness, but if I were a citizen where they prevail I would do my best to get a title, for the consideration it furnishes – that is what we want. In Republics we strive for it with the surest means we have – money.

– Notebook #40, Jan. 1897-July 1900

NUDITY

I judge that the first thing a statue dug up in the Campagna does is to go shopping & buy an offensive & obscene fig leaf. Imagine him cheapening the article at the counter & contriving how to take the innocence out of his nakedness & make the latter most offensive & conspicuous. Animals with fig leaf under tail.

– Notebook #17, Oct. 1878-Feb. 1879

So it is not nakedness that gives the sense of immodesty, the modifying the nakedness is what does it.

– passage omitted from A Tramp Abroad,
Mark Twain's Notebooks & Journals, Vol. 2

OBSCENITY

Indecency, vulgarity, obscenity – these are strictly confined to man; he invented them. Among the higher animals there is no trace of them.

– The Lowest Animal

OBSCURITY

Obscurity and a competence. That is the life that is best worth living.

– Notebook

ONANISM

Of all the kinds of sexual intercourse, this has least to recommend it. As an amusement it is too fleeting, as an occupation it is too wearing; as a public exhibition there is no money in it. It has, in our last day of progress and improvement, been degraded to brotherhood with flatulence – among the best bred these two arts are now indulged only in private – though by consent of the whole company, when only males are present, it is still permissible, in good society, to remove the embargo upon the fundamental sigh.

– *Some Thoughts on the Science of Onanism* speech, 1879

Caesar in his *Commentaries*, says, "to the lonely it is company; to the forsaken it is a friend; to the aged and impotent it is a benefactor; they that be penniless are yet rich, in that they still have this majestic diversion. There are times when I prefer it to sodomy."

– *Some Thoughts on the Science of Onanism* speech, 1879

The monkey is the only animal, except man, that practices this science; hence he is our brother; there is a bond of sympathy and relationship between us. Give this ingenious animal an audience of the proper kind, and he will straightway put aside his other affairs and take a whet; and you will see by the contortions and his ecstatic expression that he takes an intelligent and human interest in his performance.

– *Some Thoughts on the Science of Onanism* speech, 1879

OPERA

... there isn't often anything in Wagner opera that one would call by such a violent name as acting; as a rule all you would see would be a couple of ... .people, one of them standing, the other catching flies. Of course I do not really mean that he would be catching flies; I only mean that the usual operatic gestures which consist in reaching first one hand out into the air then the other might suggest the sport I speak of if the operator attended strictly to business ...

– *The Shrine of St. Wagner*

Wagner's music is better than it sounds.
> – *Autobiography of Mark Twain* (re-quoting humorist Bill Nye)

OPINION

When we are young we generally estimate an opinion by the size of the person that holds it, but later we find that is an uncertain rule, for we realize that there are times when a hornet's opinion disturbs us more than an emperor's.
> – An Undelivered Speech, March 25, 1895

OPPORTUNITY

I was seldom able to see an opportunity until it had ceased to be one.
> – *Autobiography of Mark Twain*

OPTIMISM

At 50 a man can be an ass without being an optimist but not an optimist without being an ass
> – *More Maxims of Mark*, Merle Johnson, 1927.

Optimist: day dreamer more elegantly spelled.
> – *More Maxims of Mark*, Merle Johnson, 1927

Optimist: day-dreamer in his small clothes.
> – *More Maxims of Mark*, Merle Johnson, 1927

Optimist: person who travels on nothing from nowhere to happiness.
> – *More Maxims of Mark*, Merle Johnson, 1927

It is a dear and lovely disposition, and a most valuable one, that can brush away indignities and discourtesies and seek and find the pleasanter features of an experience.
> – *Autobiography of Mark Twain*

That optimist of yours is always ready to turn hell's back yard into a play-ground.
> – *Mark Twain, a Biography*

71

... fry me an optimist for breakfast.
                          – Letter to Thomas B. Aldrich, Dec. 21, 1901

ORIGINALITY

What a good thing Adam had – when he said a good thing, he knew nobody had said it before.
                                                              – *Notebook*

PALM TREE

Nature's imitation of an umbrella that has been out to see what a cyclone is like and is trying not to look disappointed.
                                              – *Following the Equator*

PARDONS

I have had no experience in making laws or amending them, but still I cannot understand why, when it takes twelve men to inflict the death penalty upon a person, it should take any less than twelve more to undo their work. If I were a legislature, & had just been elected & had not had time to sell out, I would put the pardoning & commuting power into the hands of twelve able men instead of dumping so huge a burden upon the shoulders of one poor petition-persecuted individual.
                              – Letter to Whitelaw Reid, March 7, 1873

PARENTS

Always obey your parents, when they are present. Most parents think they know more than you do; and you can generally make more by humoring that superstition than you can by acting on your own better judgement.
                                    – *Advice to Youth*, April 15, 1882

PAST

I said there was but one solitary thing about the past worth remembering and that was the fact that it is past – can't be restored.
                                – Letter to Mr. Burrough, Nov. 1, 1876

For the majority of us, the past is a regret, the future an experiment
> – Quoted in *Mark Twain and I*, Opie Read

PATIENCE

All good things arrive unto them that wait – and don't die in the meantime.
> – Letter to Orion and Jane Clemens, April 3, 1889

PATRIOTISM

Patriotism is usually the refuge of the scoundrel. He is the man who talks the loudest.
> – *Education and Citizenship* speech, May 14, 1908
> [In the first sentence, Twain is paraphrasing Samuel Johnson.]

Patriot: the person who can holler the loudest without knowing what he is hollering about.
> – *More Maxims of Mark*, Merle Johnson, 1927

PAUSE

No word was ever as effective as a rightly timed pause.
> – *Mark Twain's Speeches*

That impressive silence, that eloquent silence, that geometrically progressive silence which often achieves a desired effect where no combination of words howsoever felicitous could accomplish it.
> – *Autobiography of Mark Twain*

PEACE

Peace by persuasion has a pleasant sound, but I think we should not be able to work it. We should have to tame the human race first, and history seems to show that that cannot be done.
> – Letter to William T. Stead, Jan. 9, 1899

PENNSYLVANIA

Wm. Penn achieved the deathless gratitude of the savage by merely dealing in a square way with them – well, kind of a square way, anyhow – more rectangular than the savage was used to, at any rate. He bought the whole State of Pa. from them & paid for it like a man. Paid $40 worth of glass beads & a couple of second-hand blankets. Bought the whole State for that. Why you can't buy its legislature for twice the money now.

– Notebook, Aug. 1890-June 1891

PERSPECTIVE

Consider well the proportion of things. It is better to be a young June – bug than an old bird of paradise.

– Pudd'nhead Wilson's Calendar

PESSIMISM

It is easy to find fault, if one has that disposition. There was once a man who, not being able to find any other fault with his coal, complained that there were too many prehistoric toads in it.

– Pudd'nhead Wilson

There is no sadder sight than a young pessimist, except an old optimist.

– Notebook, 1902-1903

... the man who isn't a pessimist is a damned fool.

– Mark Twain, a Biography

The man who is a pessimist before 48 knows too much; if he is an optimist after it, he knows too little.

– Notebook, 1902-1903

PHILOSOPHY

Every man is in his own person the whole human race without

a detail lacking ...I knew I should not find in any philosophy a single thought which had not passed through my own head, nor a single thought which had not passed through the heads of millions and millions of men before I was born.

– Mark Twain in Eruption

PHYSICIANS

The physician's is the highest and worthiest of all occupations, or would be if human nature did not make supersititons and priests necessary.

– Notebook #20, Jan. 1882-Feb. 1883

A half-educated physician is not valuable. He thinks he can cure everything.

– Notebook

PILOTING

A pilot, in those days, was the only unfettered and entirely independent human being that lived in the earth.

– Life on the Mississippi

I wish I was back there piloting up & down the river again. Verily, all is vanity and little worth – save piloting.

– Letter to Jane Clemens, Oct. 1865

Piloting on the Mississippi River was not work to me; it was play – delightful play, vigorous play, adventurous play – and I loved it.

– Mark Twain in Eruption

PIRATES

Now and then we had a hope that if we lived and were good, God would permit us to be pirates.

– Life on the Mississippi

PLAGIARISM

Nothing is ours but our language, our phrasing. If a man takes that from me (knowingly, purposely) he is a thief. If he takes it unconsciously – snaking it out of some old secluded corner of his memory, and mistaking it for a new birth instead of a mummy – he is no thief, and no man has a case against him. Unconscious appropriation is utterly common; it is not plagiarism and is no crime; but conscious appropriation, i. e., plagiarism, is as rare as parricide.

– Letter to Robert Burdette, [circa] April 19, 1890

I know one thing – that a certain amount of pride always goes along with a teaspoonful of brains, and that this pride protects a man from deliberately stealing other people's ideas. That is what a teaspoonful of brains will do for a man – and admirers had often told me I had nearly a basketful – though they were rather reserved as to the size of the basket.

– *Unconscious Plagiarism* speech

PLEDGE

... to make a pledge of any kind is to declare war against nature; for a pledge is a chain that is always clanking and reminding the wearer of it that he is not a free man.

– *Following the Equator*

PLUMBER

When we were finishing our house, we found we had a little cash left over, on account of the plumber not knowing it.

– *The McWilliamses and the Burglar Alarm*

POLITICS

… the citizen who thinks he sees that the commonwealth's political clothes are worn out, and yet holds his peace and does not agitate for a new suit, is disloyal; he is a traitor.

– *A Connecticut Yankee in King Arthur's Court*

POETRY

What a lumbering poor vehicle prose is for the conveying of a great thought! ... Prose wanders around with a lantern & laboriously schedules & verifies the details & particulars of a valley & its frame of crags & peaks, then Poetry comes, & lays bare the whole landscape with a single splendid flash.
– Letter to W. D. Howells, Feb. 25, 1906

Anybody can write the first line of a poem, but it is a very difficult task to make the second line rhyme with the first.
– Speech, Sept 23, 1907

I have thought many times since that if poets when they get discouraged would blow their brains out, they could write very much better when they got well.
– Speech in Liverpool, England July 10, 1907

POKER

There are few things that are so unpardonably neglected in our country as poker. The upper class knows very little about it. Now and then you find ambassadors who have sort of a general knowledge of the game, but the ignorance of the people is fearful. Why, I have known clergymen, good men, kind-hearted, liberal, sincere, and all that, who did not know the meaning of a "flush." It is enough to make one ashamed of one's species.
– Quoted in *A Bibliography of Mark Twain*, Merle Johnson, 1935

POLITICS

The political and commercial morals of the United States are not merely food for laughter, they are an entire banquet.
– *Mark Twain in Eruption*

No matter how healthy a man's morals may be when he enters the White House, he comes out again with a pot-marked soul.
– Quoted in *My Father Mark Twain*, Clara Clemens

An honest man in politics shines more there than he would elsewhere.

– A Tramp Abroad

The new political gospel: public office is private graft.
– More Maxims of Mark, Merle Johnson, 1927

POPULARITY

The more things are forbidden, the more popular they become.
– Notebook, 1895

Everybody's private motto: It's better to be popular than right.
– Notebook, 1902

Even popularity can be overdone. In Rome, along at first, you are full of regrets that Michelangelo died; but by and by you only regret that you didn't see him do it.

– Pudd'nhead Wilson's Calendar

POVERTY

He is now fast rising from affluence to poverty.
– Henry Ward Beecher's Farm, 1885

PRAYER

It is better to read the weather forecast before we pray for rain.
– Notebook; also quoted in *More Maxims of Mark*,
Merle Johnson, 1927

[Man] prays for help, and favor, and protection, every day; and does it with hopefulness and confidence, too, although no prayer of his has ever been answered. The daily affront, the daily defeat, do not discourage him, he goes on praying just the same.

– Satan's Letter I, Letters from the Earth

PREACHERS

Preachers are always pleasant company when they are off duty.
– Letter to San Francisco *Alta California*, written
April 30, 1867; published June 10, 1867

PRIESTS

Man is so made that he eagerly wants to know; whereas the priest, like God, whose imitator and representative he is, has made it his business from the beginning to keep him from knowing any useful thing.
– *Satan's Letter III, Letters from the Earth*

PRINCE AND THE PAUPER, THE

If I knew it would never sell a copy my jubilant delight in writing it would not suffer any diminution.
– Letter to W. D. Howells, March 5, 1880

PRINCIPLES

You cannot have a theory without principles. Principles is another name for prejudices.
– *Literature* speech

Prosperity is the best protector of principle.
– *Following the Equator*

We all live in the protection of certain cowardices which we call our principles.
– *More Maxims of Mark*, Merle Johnson, 1927

"I was obliged to eat [apples], I was so hungry. It was against my principles, but I find that principles have no real force except when one is well fed..."
– *Adams's Diary*

Principles aren't of much account, anyway, except at election time. After that you hang them up to let them season.
– *The Anti-doughnut Party* speech, 1901

PROCRASTINATION

Do not put off until tomorrow what can be put off till day-after-tomorrow just as well.
                                    – *More Maxims of Mark*, Merle Johnson, 1927

Let us save tomorrows for work.
                                    – *More Maxims of Mark*, Merle Johnson, 1927

PROFANITY

Let us swear while we may, for in Heaven it will not be allowed.
                                    – *Notebook*, 1898

If I cannot swear in heaven I shall not stay there.
                                    – Notebook, 1898

... he was empty. You could have drawn a [fishing net[through his system and not caught curses enough to disturb your mother.
                                    – *Life on the Mississippi*

I was ... blaspheming my luck in a way that made my breath smell of brimstone.
                                    – *Roughing It*

... quadrilateral, astronomical, incandescent son-of-a-bitch.
                                    – Letter to W. D. Howells, (attacking an enemy)

The idea that no gentleman ever swears is all wrong. He can swear and still be a gentleman if he does it in a nice and be-nevolent and affectionate way.
                                    – *Private and Public Morals* speech, 1906

When angry count four; when very angry, swear.
                                    – *Pudd'nhead Wilson's Calendar*

There ought to be a room in every house to swear in. It's dangerous to have to repress an emotion like that.
                                    – *Mark Twain, a Biography*

Under certain circumstances, urgent circumstances, desperate circumstances, profanity provides a relief denied even to prayer.
— *Mark Twain, a Biography*

PROMISES

To promise not to do a thing is the surest way in the world to make a body want to go and do that very thing.
— *Adventures of Tom Sawyer*

Better a broken promise than none at all.
— *More Maxims of Mark*, Merle Johnson, 1927

PROOFREADERS

Yesterday Mr. Hall wrote that the printer's proof-reader was improving my punctuation for me, & I telegraphed orders to have him shot without giving him time to pray.
— Letter, 1889

In the first place God made idiots. This was for practice. Then he made proof-readers.
— 1893

PROPORTION

It's a matter of proportion, that's what it is; and when you come to gauge a thing's speed by its size, where's your bird and your man and your railroad alongside of a flea? ... A flea is just a comet, b'iled down small.
— *Tom Sawyer Abroad*

PROVIDENCE

There are many scapegoats for our blunders, but the most popular one is Providence.
— *Notebook*, 1898

PUBLIC OPINION

That awful power, the public opinion of a nation, is created in America by a horde of ignorant, self-complacent who failed at ditching and shoemaking and fetched up in journalism on their way to the poorhouse.

– License of the Press speech

PUBLISHERS

With ever increasing affection (when you do as I tell you).
– Letter to publisher Chatto & Windus, June 28, 1898

All publishers are Columbuses. The successful author is their America. The reflection that they – like Columbus – didn't discover what they expected to discover, and didn't discover what they started out to discover, doesn't trouble them. All they remember is that they discovered America; they forget that they started out to discover some patch or corner of India.

– Mark Twain in Eruption

Robbery of a publisher – I said that if he regarded that as a crime it was because his education was limited. I said it was not a crime and was always rewarded in heaven with two halos. Would be, if it ever happened.

– Mark Twain in Eruption

PUN

... no circumstances, however dismal, will ever be considered a sufficient excuse for the admission of that last and saddest evidence of intellectual poverty, the Pun.

– Mark Twain, a Biography

PUNISHMENT

Very well, God banished Adam and Eve from the Garden, and eventually assassinated them. All for disobeying a command which he had no right to utter. But he did not stop there, as you will see. He has one code of morals for himself, and quite another for his children. He requires his children to deal justly – and gently – with offenders, and forgive them seventy-and-seven times; whereas he deals neither justly nor gently with anyone, and he did not forgive the ignorant and thoughtless first pair of juveniles even their first small offense and say, "You may go free this time, and I will give you another chance." On the contrary! He elected to punish their children, all through the ages to the end of time, for a trifling offense committed by others before they were born. He is punishing them yet. In mild ways? No, in atrocious ones.

– *Satan's Letter III, Letters from the Earth*

QUOTATION

It is my belief that nearly any invented quotation, played with confidence, stands a good chance to deceive.

– *Following the Equator*

RADICAL

The radical of one century is the conservative of the next. The radical invents the views. When he has worn them out the conservative adopts them.

– *Notebook*, 1898

RAFT

We said there warn't no home like a raft, after all. Other places do seem so cramped up and smothery, but a raft don't. You feel mighty free and easy and comfortable on a raft.

– *Adventures of Huckleberry Finn, Ch. 18*

RAILROAD

A railroad is like a lie – you have to keep building to it to make it stand.

– Letter to the San Francisco *Alta California*,
published May 26, 1867

RAIN

The rain is famous for falling on the just and unjust alike, but if I had the management of such affairs I would rain softly and sweetly on the just, but if I caught a sample of the unjust out doors I would drown him.

– Quoted in *My Father Mark Twain*, Clara Clemens

It is better to read the weather forecast before we pray for rain.
– *Notebook*; also quoted in *More Maxims of Mark,*
Merle Johnson, 1927

RAINBOW

We have not the reverent feeling for the rainbow that the savage has, because we know how it is made. We have lost as much as we gained by prying into that matter.

– *A Tramp Abroad*

READING

I don't believe any of you have ever read *Paradise Lost*, and you don't want to. That's something that you just want to take on trust. It's a classic ... something that everybody wants to have read and nobody wants to read.

– *Disappearance of Literature* speech

Be careful about reading health books. You may die of a misprint. Classic – a book which people praise and don't read.
– *Pudd'nhead Wilson's New Calendar*

When I am king, they shall not have bread and shelter only, but also teachings out of books, for a full belly is little worth where the mind is starved.

– *The Prince and the Pauper*

I had rather you read fifty *Jumping Frogs* than one *Don Quixote*. *Don Quixote* is one of the most exquisite books that was ever written, and to lose it from the world's literature would be as the wresting of a constellation from the symmetry and perfection of the firmament – but neither it nor Shakespeare are proper books for virgins to read until some hand has culled them of their grossness.

– Letter to Olivia Clemens, March 1, 1869

REASON

Man is the Reasoning Animal. Such is the claim. I think it is open to dispute.

– The Lowest Animal

The thug is aware that loudness convinces sixty persons where reasoning convinces but one.

– Is Shakespeare Dead?

REDHEADS

When red-headed people are above a certain social grade their hair is auburn.

– A Connecticut Yankee in King Arthur's Court

RELIGION

So much blood has been shed by the Church because of an omission from the Gospel: "Ye shall be indifferent as to what your neighbor's religion is." Not merely tolerant of it, but indifferent to it. Divinity is claimed for many religions; but no religion is great enough or divine enough to add that new law to its code.

– Mark Twain, a Biography

Peace of mind is a most valuable thing. The Bible has robbed the majority of the world of it during many centuries; it is but fair that in return it should give some to an individual here & there. But you must not make the mistake of supposing that absolute peace of mind is obtainable only through some form religious belief: no, on the contrary I have found that as perfect a peace is to be found in absolute unbelief.

– Letter to Charles W. Stoddard, June 1, 1885

But we were good boys ... we didn't break the Sabbath often enough to signify – once a week perhaps... Anyway, we were good Presbyterian boys when the weather was doubtful; when it was fair, we did wander a little from the fold.

– 67th Birthday speech

I was educated, I was trained, I was a Presbyterian and I knew how these things are done. I knew that in Biblical times if a man committed a sin the extermination of the whole surrounding nation – cattle and all – was likely to happen. I knew that Providence was not particular about the rest, so that He got somebody connected with the one He was after.

– Autobiography of Mark Twain

We despise all reverences and all the objects of reverence which are outside the pale of our own list of sacred things. And yet, with strange inconsistency, we are shocked when other people despise and defile the things which are holy to us.

– Following the Equator

Man is a Religious Animal. He is the only Religious Animal. He is the only animal that has the True Religion – several of them. He is the only animal that loves his neighbor as himself and cuts his throat if his theology isn't straight. He has made a graveyard of the globe in trying his honest best to smooth his brother's path to happiness and heaven. ... The higher animals have no religion. And we are told that they are going to be left out in the Hereafter. I wonder why? It seems questionable taste.

– The Lowest Animal

India has two million gods, and worships them all. In religion all other countries are paupers; India is the only millionaire.

– Following the Equator

REPENTANCE

I never did a thing in all my life, virtuous or otherwise that I didn't repent of within twenty-four hours.

– The Facts Concerning the Recent Carnival Crime in Connecticut

REPUTATION

Reputation is a hall-mark: it can remove doubt from pure silver, and it can also make the plated article pass for pure.

– Unmailed letter, 1886

RESPECT

Be respectful to your superiors, if you have any; also to strangers, and sometimes to others. If a person offends you, and you are in doubt as to whether it was intentional or not, do not resort to extreme measure; simply watch your chance and hit him with a brick. That will be sufficient. If you shall find that he had not intended any offense, come out frankly and confess yourself in the wrong when you struck him; acknowledge it like a man, and say you didn't mean to.

– *Advice to Youth, May 15, 1882*

We are all inconsistent. We are offended and resent it when people do not respect us; and yet in his private heart no man much respects himself.

– *Following the Equator*

RETREATING

I could have become a soldier if I had waited; I knew more about retreating than the man who invented retreating.

— *Private History of a Campaign That Failed*

REVENGE

Revenge is wicked, & unchristian & in every way unbecoming, & I am not the man to countenance it or show it any favor. (But it is powerful sweet, anyway.)

– Letter to Olivia Clemens, Dec. 27, 1869

REVOLUTION

No people in the world ever did achieve their freedom by goody-goody talk and moral suasion: it being immutable law that all revolutions that will succeed must being in blood, whatever may answer afterward.

– A Connecticut Yankee in King Arthur's Court

RIDICULE

No god and no religion can survive ridicule. No church, no nobility, no royalty or other fraud, can face ridicule in a fair field and live.

– Notebook, 1888

RIGHT

Always do right; this will gratify some people and astonish the rest.

– Note to the Young People's Society,
Greenpoint Presbyterian Church, 1901

Do right and you will be conspicuous.

– Mark Twain, a Biography

Do right for your own sake and be happy in knowing that your neighbor will certainly share in the benefits resulting.

– What Is Man?

What's the use you learning to do right when it's troublesome to do right and ain't no trouble to do wrong, and the wages is just the same?

– Adventures of Huckleberry Finn

ROBBERY

A robber is much more high-toned than what a pirate is – as a general thing. In most countries they're awful high up in the nobility – dukes and such.

– Adventures of Tom Sawyer

Man is the only animal that robs his helpless fellow of his country – takes possession of it and drives him out of it or destroys him. Man has done this in all the ages. There is not an acre of ground on the globe that is in possession of its rightful owner, or that has not been taken away from owner after owner, cycle after cycle, by force and bloodshed.

– The Lowest Animal

ROMANCE

The romance of life is the only part of it which is overwhelmingly valuable, and romance dies with youth. After that, life is a drudge, & indeed a sham.

– Letter to Will Bowen, June 6, 1900

ROOSEVELT, TEDDY

Mr. Roosevelt is the Tom Sawyer of the political world of the twentieth century; always showing off; always hunting for a chance to show off; in his frenzied imagination the Great Republic is a vast Barnum circus with him for a clown and the whole world for audience; he would go to Halifax for half a chance to show off and he would go to hell for a whole one.

– Mark Twain in Eruption

ROYALTY

There never was a throne which did not represent a crime.

– Mark Twain, a Biography

The institution of royalty in any form is an insult to the human race.

– Notebook, 1888

RULES

It is good to obey all the rules when you're young, so you'll have the strength to break them when you're old.

– Quoted by Dorothy Quick in Advance magazine, Feb. 1940

ST. LOUIS

If you send a damned fool to St. Louis, and you don't tell them he's a damned fool, they'll never find out.

– Life on the Mississippi

SATAN

But who prays for Satan? Who in eighteen centuries, has had the common humanity to pray for the one sinner that needed it most, our one fellow and brother who most needed a friend yet had not a single one, the one sinner among us all who had the highest and clearest right to every Christian's daily and nightly prayers, for the plain and unassailable reason that his was the first and greatest need, he being among sinners the supremest?

– Autobiography of Mark Twain

SAVAGES

There are many humorous things in the world: among them the white man's notion that he is less savage than the other savages.

– Following the Equator

The only very marked difference between the average civilized man and the average savage is that the one is gilded and the other is painted.

– Notebook

SCIENCE

There is something fascinating about science. One gets such wholesale returns of conjecture out of such a trifling investment of fact.

– Life on the Mississippi

SELF-ESTEEM

... we do not deal much in fact when we are contemplating ourselves.

– Does the Race of Man Love a Lord?

It shames the average man to be valued below his own estimate of his worth.

– A Connecticut Yankee in King Arthur's Court

SEXUAL INTERCOURSE

For there is nothing about man that is not strange to an immortal. He looks at nothing as we look at it, his sense of proportion is quite different from ours, and his sense of values is so widely divergent from ours, that with all our large intellectual powers it is not likely that even the most gifted among us would ever be quite able to understand it.

For instance, take this sample: he has imagined a heaven, and has left entirely out of it the supremest of all his delights, the one ecstasy that stands first and foremost in the heart of every individual of his race – and of ours – sexual intercourse! It is as if a lost and perishing person in a roasting desert should be told by a rescuer he might choose and have all longed-for things but one, and he should elect to leave out water!

– Satan's Letter II, Letters from the Earth

So the First Pair went forth from the Garden under a curse – a permanent one. They had lost every pleasure they had possessed before "The Fall"; and yet they were rich, for they had gained one worth all the rest: they knew the Supreme Art. They practiced it diligently and were filled with contentment. The Deity ordered them to practice it. They obeyed, this time. But it was just as well it was not forbidden, for they would have practiced it anyhow, if a thousand Deities had forbidden it. Results followed. By the name of Cain and Abel. And these had some sisters; and knew what to do with them. And so there were some more results: Cain and Abel begot some nephews and nieces. These, in their turn, begot some second cousins. At this point classification of relationships began to get difficult, and the attempt to keep it up was abandoned.

– Satan's Letter IV, Letters from the Earth

SKATING

There would be a power of fun in skating if you could do it with somebody else's muscles.

– Letter to Thomas B. Aldrich, Dec. 18, 1874

When you are on skates you waddle off as stuffy and stupid and ungainly as a buzzard that's had half a horse for dinner.

*– Curtain Lecture on Skating, New York
Sunday Mercury, March 17, 1867*

SLANDER

It takes your enemy and your friend, working together, to hurt you to the heart; the one to slander you and the other to get the news to you.

– Following the Equator

SLOWNESS

I have seen slower people than I am – and more deliberate ... and even quieter, and more listless, and lazier people than I am. But they were dead.

– Memoranda, Galaxy magazine, Dec. 1870

SMOKING

As an example to others, and not that I care for moderation myself, it has always been my rule never to smoke when asleep and never to refrain when awake.

– 70th Birthday speech

SNORING

A use has been found for everything but snoring.

– Notebook, May 1892-Jan. 1893

There ain't no way to find out why a snorer can't hear himself snore.

– Tom Sawyer Abroad

SOUL

Be careless in your dress if you must, but keep a tidy soul.
– Following the Equator

SPECTACLES

It was on the 10th day of May 1884 that I confessed to age by mounting spectacles for the first time, and in the same hour I renewed my youth, to outward appearance, by mounting a bicycle for the first time. The spectacles stayed on.
– Mark Twain's Speeches

SPECULATION

There are two times in a man's life when he should not speculate: when he can't afford it and when he can.
– Following the Equator

SPELLING

They spell it Vinci and pronounce it Vinchy; foreigners always spell better than they pronounce.
– The Innocents Abroad

... simplified spelling is all right, but, like chastity, you can carry it too far.
– The Alphabet and Simplified Spelling speech, Dec. 9, 1907

STATESMANSHIP

If we had less statesmanship, we would get along with fewer battleships.
– Notebook, 1905

STEALING

It is better to take what does not belong to you than to let it lie around neglected.
– More Maxims of Mark, Merle Johnson, 1927

You ought never to take anything that don't belong to you – if you cannot carry it off.

– Advice for Good Little Boys

STORY

I like a good story well told. That is the reason I am sometimes forced to tell them myself.

– Watermelon speech, 1907

STUPIDITY

[He] was endowed with a stupidity which by the least little stretch would go around the globe four times and tie.

– Mark Twain in Eruption

SUCCESS

Behold the fool saith, "Put not all thine eggs in the one basket" – which is but a manner of saying, "Scatter your money and your attention;" but the wise man saith, "Put all your eggs in the one basket and – WATCH THAT BASKET."

– Pudd'nHead Wilson

All you need in this life is ignorance and confidence, and then Success is sure.

– Notebook, 1887

SUNDAY

The day of rest comes but once a week, and sorry am I that it does not come oftener. Man is so constituted that he can stand more rest than this. I often think regretfully that it would have been so easy to have two Sundays in a week, and yet it was not so ordained. The omnipotent Creator could have made the world in three days just as easily as he made it in six, and this would have doubled the Sundays. Still it is not our place to criticize the wisdom of the Creator.

– Reflections on the Sabbath

As you have seen, that singular show is a service of praise: praise by hymn, praise by prostration. It takes the place of "church." Now then, in the earth these people cannot stand much church – an hour and a quarter is the limit, and they draw the line at once a week. That is to say, Sunday. One day in seven; and even then they do not look forward to it with longing. And so – consider what their heaven provides for them: "church" that lasts forever, and a Sabbath that has no end! They quickly weary of this brief hebdomadal Sabbath here, yet they long for that eternal one; they dream of it, they talk about it, they *think* they think they are going to enjoy it – with all their simple hearts they think they think they are going to be happy in it!

– Satan's Letter II, Letters from the Earth

SUPREMACY

Some instinct tells me that eternal vigilance is the price of supremacy.

– Eve's Diary

SURGEONS

It is a gratification to me to know that I am ignorant of art, and ignorant also of surgery. Because people who understand art find nothing in pictures but blemishes, and surgeons and anatomists see no beautiful women in all their lives, but only a ghastly stack of bones with Latin names to them, and a network of nerves and muscles and tissues.

– Letter to San Francisco *Alta California*, dated May 28, 1867; published July 28, 1867

TALENT

To spell correctly is a talent, not an acquirement. There is some dignity about an acquirement, because it is a product of your own labor. It is wages earned, whereas to be able to do a thing merely by the grace of God and not by your own effort transfers the distinction to our heavenly home – where possibly it is a matter of pride and satisfaction but it leaves you naked and bankrupt.

– Autobiography of Mark Twain

We are always more anxious to be distinguished for a talent which we do not possess, than to be praised for the fifteen which we do possess.

– Autobiography of Mark Twain; also quoted in
More Maxims of Mark, Merle Johnson, 1927

TAXES

What is the difference between a taxidermist and a tax collector? The taxidermist takes only your skin.

– Notebook, 1902

TEMPER

It takes me a long time to lose my temper, but once lost I could not find it with a dog.

– Notebook, 1894

... there is not another temper as bad as mine except God Almighty's.

– Letter to W. D. Howells, Oct. 19, 1899

TEMPERANCE

Temperate temperance is best. Intemperate temperance injures the cause of temperance, while temperate temperance helps it in its fight against intemperate intemperance. Fanatics will never learn that, though it be written in letters of gold across the sky.

– Notebook, 1896

What marriage is to morality, a properly conducted licensed liquor traffic is to sobriety. In fact, the more things are forbidden, the more popular they become.

– Notebook, 1895

It is the prohibition that makes anything precious.

– Notebook

TOLERANCE

All the talk about tolerance, in anything or anywhere, is plainly a gentle lie. It does not exist. It is in no man's heart; but it unconsciously, and by moss-grown inherited habit, drivels and slobbers from all men's lips.

– Autobiography of Mark Twain

If the man doesn't believe as we do, we say he is a crank and that settles it. I mean it does nowadays, because we can't burn him.

– Following the Equator

TRUTH

Familiarity breeds contempt. How accurate that is. The reason we hold truth in such respect is because we have so little opportunity to get familiar with it.

– Notebook

I have not professionally dealt in truth. Many when they come to die have spent all the truth that was in them, and enter the next world as paupers. I have saved up enough to make an astonishment there.

– Notebook

No real gentleman will tell the naked truth in the presence of ladies.

– A Double-Barreled Detective Story

TYPEWRITER

[Editor's note: Twain was excited by the typewriter on first seeing one in Boston in 1874. Shortly thereafter he bought one and started practising on it, before later giving up in frustration. He typed his first letter to his brother, Orion, and his second to his friend William Dean Howells. Here is the letter to Howells, (complete with typos).]

You neednt alswer this; I am only practicing to get three; anothe slip-up there; only practici?ng ti get the hang of the thing. I notice I miss fire & get in a good many unnecessary

97

letters & punctuation marks. I am simply using you for a target to bang at. Blame my cats, but this thing requires genius in order to work it just right.

> – Letter to W.D. Howells, Dec. 9, 1874

[Twain bartered the typewriter to his friend Frank Bliss, for a $12 saddle ("cheating him outrageously," Twain said. Bliss later returned the machine and Twain gave it to Howells.]

I will now claim – until dispossessed – that I was the first person in the world to apply the typewriter to literature... The early machine was full of caprices, full of defects – devilish ones. It had as many immoralities as the machine of today has virtues. After a year or two I found that it was degrading my character, so I thought I would give it to Howells ... He took it home to Boston, and my morals began to improve, but his have never recovered.

> – *The First Writing Machines*

UNDERTAKER

Let us endeavor so to live that when we come to die even the undertaker will be sorry.

> – *Puddn'head Wilson's Calendar*

We must take the position that burial is stuck to merely in the interest of the undertaker (who has his family cremated to save expense).

> – Marginalia in C. F. Gordon-Cumming's book
> *In the Himalayas and on the Indian Plains*

VANITY

There are no grades of vanity, there are only grades of ability in concealing it.

> – *Notebook*, 1898

VICES
I haven't a particle of confidence in a man who has no redeeming petty vices.

> – *Mark Twain, a Biography*

VIRTUE

The weakest of all weak things is a virtue that has not been tested in the fire.

– The Man That Corrupted Hadleyburg

Be virtuous and you will be eccentric.

– Mental Photographs, A Curious Dream, 1872

VOCATIONS

I had gained a livelihood in various vocations, but had not dazzled anybody with my successes; still the list was before me, and the amplest liberty in the matter of choosing, provided I wanted to work – which I did not, after being so wealthy. I had once been a grocery clerk, for one day, but had consumed so much sugar in that time that I was relieved from further duty by the proprietor; said he wanted me outside, so that he could have my custom. I had studied law an entire week, and then given it up because it was so prosy and tiresome. I had engaged briefly in the study of blacksmithing, but wasted so much time trying to fix the bellows so that it would blow itself, that the master turned me adrift in disgrace, and told me I would come to no good. I had been a bookseller's clerk for awhile, but the customers bothered me so much I could not read with any comfort, and so the proprietor gave me a furlough and forgot to put a limit to it. I had clerked in a drug store part of a summer, but my prescriptions were unlucky, and we appeared to sell more stomach pumps than soda water. So I had to go. I had made of myself a tolerable printer, under the impression that I would be another Franklin some day, but somehow had missed the connection thus far.

– Roughing It

VILLAGE

Human nature cannot be studied in cities except at a disadvantage – a village is the place. There you can know your man inside and out – in a city you but know his crust; and his crust is usually a lie.

– Notebook, 1883

VOTE

Vote: the only commodity that is peddleable without a license.
— *More Maxims of Mark*, Merle Johnson, 1927

VULGAR

There are no people who are quite so vulgar as the over-refined.
— *Following the Equator*

WAR

All war must be just the killing of strangers against whom you feel no personal animosity; strangers whom, in other circumstances, you would help if you found them in trouble, and who would help you if you needed it.
— *The Private History of the Campaign That Failed*

Before I had chance in another war, the desire to kill people to whom I had not been introduced had passed away.
— *Autobiography of Mark Twain*

A wanton waste of projectiles.
— *The Art of War* speech, 1881

WASHINGTON, D.C.

There is something good and motherly about Washington, the grand old benevolent National Asylum for the helpless.
— *The Gilded Age*

WASHINGTON, GEORGE

He was ignorant of the commonest accomplishments of youth. He would not even lie.
— Column in Virginia City *Territorial Enterprise*, Feb. 1866

That George could refrain from telling the lie is not the remarkable feature, but that he could do it off-hand that way.
— *More Maxims of Mark*, Merle Johnson, 1927

I am different from Washington; I have a higher, gr
ard of principle. Washington could not lie. I can lie, b
– Quoted in *Mark Twain*, Archibald He

WEALTH

Being rich ain't what it's cracked up to be. It's just worry and
worry, and sweat and sweat, and a-wishing you was dead all
the time.

– *The Adventures of Tom Sawyer*

WIT

Wit is the sudden marriage of ideas which, before their union,
were not perceived to have any relation.

– *Notebook*, 1885

WOMEN

There is nothing comparable to the endurance of a woman. In
military life she would tire out an army of men, either in camp
or on the march.

– *Autobiography of Mark Twain*

Some civilized women would lose half their charm without
dress; and some would lose all of it.

– *Woman, God Bless Her* speech

What, Sir, would the people of the earth be without woman?
They would be scarce, sir, almighty scarce.

– Speech, Nov. 11, 1868

The reason novelists nearly always fail in depicting women
when they make them act, is that they let them do what they
have observed some woman has done at some time or another. And that is where they make a mistake; for a woman
will never do again what has been done before.

– *The Gilded Age*

WORDS

pital. We can invest it or we can squan-

– Notebook, 1898

e almost right word & the right word
t's the difference between the light-
g and the lightning.

– Letter to George Bainton, 1888

The right word may be effective, but no word was ever as effective as a rightly timed pause.

– Mark Twain's Speeches

Use the right word, not its second cousin.

– Fenimore Cooper's Literary Offences, 1895

A powerful agent is the right word. Whenever we come upon
one of those intensely right words in a book or a newspaper
the resulting effect is physical as well as spiritual, and electri-
cally prompt: it tingles exquisitely around through the walls
of the mouth and tastes as tart and crisp and good as the au-
tumn-butter that creams the sumac-berry.

William Dean Howells essay

WORK

I do not like work even when someone else does it.

– The Lost Napoleon

From the beginning of my sojourn in this world there was a
persistent vacancy in me where the industry ought to be.

– Autobiography of Mark Twain

Work consists of whatever a body is obliged to do. Play consists of whatever a body is not obliged to do.

– Adventures of Tom Sawyer

WRINKLES

Wrinkles should merely indicate where smiles have been.
– Following the Equator

WRITING

I have never tried, in even one single little instance, to help cultivate the cultivated classes. I was not equipped for it either by native gifts or training. And I never had any ambition in that direction, but always hunted for bigger game – the masses. I have seldom deliberately tried to instruct them, but I have done my best to entertain them, for they can get instruction elsewhere.
– Mark Twain, a Biography

Now in pleasanter days, I had amused myself with writing letters to the chief paper of the Territory, the Virginia daily *Territorial Enterprise*, and had always been surprised when they appeared in print. My good opinion of its editors had steadily declined; for it seemed to me that they might have found something better to fill up with than my literature.
– Roughing It

I conceive that the right way to write a story for boys is to write so that it will not only interest boys but strongly interest any man who has ever been a boy. That immensely enlarges the audience.
– Letter to Fred J. Hall, Aug. 10, 1892

WRONG

The fact that man knows right from wrong proves his intellectual superiority to the other creatures; but the fact that he can do wrong proves his moral inferiority to any creature that cannot.
– What Is Man?

We ought never to do wrong when people are looking.
– A Double-Barreled Detective Story

Mark Twain

Samuel Langhorne Clemens was born on Nov. 30, 1835, in Florida, Missouri, but by age four his family had moved to Hannibal, Mo., a bustling riverport town, where his childhood was very much like the one (well, without the robbers' treasure) he later portrayed in *Adventures of Tom Sawyer*. His father, a judge turned grocer, died when Sam was only 12 and he was obliged to quit school and become a printer's apprentice. He later worked for his older brother, Orion Clemens, as a typesetter, writer, editor and general dogsbody at his brother's newspaper, the *Hannibal Journal*. (Sometimes Orion would go off on business, leaving Sam in charge, and coming home to find the boy had written editorials of which Orion did not approve.)

In 1853 (he was not yet 18), Sam Clemens set off for New York and later picked up work – either as a journalist or a printer, whatever was available – in Philadelphia, Keokuk, Iowa, Cincinnatti and St. Louis. He decided to set off for adventures in South America, but became so enamored of the riverboat taking him there that he decided to train as a riverboat pilot on the Mississippi. Got quite good at it, too, until the Civil War closed the river to traffic in 1861 and he was forced to revive his journalism career.

After the war ended in 1865, U.S. president Abraham Lincoln offered Orion a job as assistant to the governor of the Nevada Territory, and Sam went along for the ride. They also tried their hand at prospecting for gold, but were not successful – the first of many failed business ventures and bad investments Sam Clemens was to endure. (Not all of Twain's business endeavors were failures. He published a biography of Ulysses S. Grant that sold quite well and helped pay off his debts.) His own books sold very well. And although he may not have invented the practice, he was a master at writing travel pieces for newspapers that helped pay his way around the world – pieces he later put together and sold again in such books as *The Innocents Abroad* and *Following the Equator*.

In Nevada, he was offered and took a job as city editor for the local newspaper, the *Territorial Enterprise*. It was here he first started using the pen name Mark Twain. (For an explanation of its origins, see the Introduction.)

In 1867, he met Olivia Langdon, the daughter of a prosperous coal merchant in New York State. (He'd met her brother on a riverboat trip.) They began courting (their first date was to hear Charles Dickens give a reading in New York City) and were married in 1870. They moved to Buffalo, N.Y., and later to Elmira, N.Y., her home town, to be closer to her family. Olivia fell ill and their first child, their son Langdon, was sickly and later died before his second birthday. Sam and his beloved Livy had three more children, all girls, though the oldest and youngest daughters died in their 20s. The middle daughter, Clara, lived to 88 and wrote a memoir of her father. They are buried in the Langdon family plot in Elmira, N.Y.

Altogether, Mark Twain wrote 28 books, as well as essays, letters, speeches, newspaper and magazine articles. He was America's first great man of letters and among the greatest – and certainly the most eminently quotable – writer America has ever produced.

Index

108

About the Editor

David W. Barber is a journalist and musician and the author of ten books of musical history and humor, including *Bach, Beethoven and the Boys, If it Ain't Baroque,* and *Tutus, Tights and Tiptoes.* He's also editor of two previous books in the Quotable series, *Quotable Alice* and *Quotable Sherlock.* Formerly entertainment editor of the Kingston, Ont., *Whig-Standard* and editor of *Broadcast Week* magazine at the Toronto *Globe and Mail,* he's now a freelance journalist and musician in Toronto. As a composer, his works include two symphonies, a jazz mass based on the music of Dave Brubeck, a *Requiem,* several short choral and chamber works and various vocal-jazz songs and arrangements. He sings with the Toronto Chamber Choir and with his vocal-jazz group, Barber & the Sevilles, which has released a CD, called *Cybersex.*

Selected Bibliography

Adventures of Huckleberry Finn, Random House © 1990
Adventures of Tom Sawyer, Random House © 1983
Autobiography of Mark Twain, ed. Charles Neider, Harper Collins © 1990
Bibliography of the Works of Mark Twain, ed.Merle Johnson Greenwood Press © 1974
Letters from the Earth, ed. Barnard Devoto, Harper & Row © 1962
Life on the Mississippi, The Heritage Press © 1944
Mark Twain, a Biography, ed. Albert Bigelow Paine, Harper & Bros © 1912
More Maxims of Mark, ed. Merle Johnson
Pudd'nhead Wilson, ComonPlace Publishing © 1997
Roughing It, University of California Press © 1972

www.twainquotes.com

Quotable Twain
© David Barber 2002

All rights reserved

Except brief excerpts for review purposes,
no part of this publication may be reproduced,
stored in a retrieval system or transmitted, in any
form or by any means, without the prior permission
of the publisher or, in the case of photocopying or
other reprographic copying, a licence from the
Canadian Reprography Collective
CANCOPY

First published in Canada by
Sound And Vision
359 Riverdale Avenue
Toronto, Canada, M4J 1A4
www.soundandvision.com

First printing, September 2002
1 3 5 7 9 - printings - 10 8 6 4 2

National Library of Canada Cataloguing in Publication

Twain, Mark, 1835-1910
Quotable Twain - compiled and edited
by David W. Barber.
Includes index.
ISBN 0-920151-56-6

1. Twain, Mark, 1835-1910—Quotations. 2. Quotations,
American.
I. Barber, David W. (David William), 1958- II. Title.
III. Series.

PS1303.B37 2002   818'.402   C2002-904218-6

Typeset in ITC Palatino
Printed and bound in Canada

Other Quotable Books

Quotable Jazz
Compiled & Edited by Marshall Bowden
Caricatures by Mike Rooth
isbn 0-920151-55-8

Quotable Pop
Fifty Decades of Blah Blah Blah
Compiled & Edited by Phil Dellio & Scott Woods
Caricatures by Mike Rooth
isbn 0-920151-50-7

Quotable Opera
Compiled & Edited by Steve & Nancy Tanner
Caricatures by Umberto Tàccola
isbn 0-920151-54-X

Quotable Alice
Compiled & Edited by David W. Barber
Illustrations by Sir John Tenniel
isbn 0-920151-52-3

Quotable Sherlock
Compiled & Edited by David W. Barber
Illustrations by Sidney Paget
isbn 0-920151-53-1

Quotable Twain
Compiled & Edited by David W. Barber
isbn 0-920151-56-6

Other books by David W. Barber
with cartoons by Dave Donald

A Musician's Dictionary
preface by Yehudi Menuhin
isbn 0-920151-21-3

Bach, Beethoven and the Boys
Music History as It Ought to Be Taught
preface by Anthony Burgess
isbn 0-920151-10-8

When the Fat Lady Sings
Opera History as It Ought to Be Taught
preface by Maureen Forrester
foreword by Anna Russell
isbn 0-920151-34-5

If It Ain't Baroque
More Music History as It Ought to Be Taught
isbn 0-920151-15-9

Getting a Handel on Messiah
preface by Trevor Pinnock
isbn 0-920151-17-5

Tenors, Tantrums and Trills
An Opera Dictionary from Aida to Zzzz
isbn 0-920151-19-1

Tutus, Tights and Tiptoes
Ballet History as It Ought to Be Taught
preface by Karen Kain
isbn 0-920151-30-2

Compiled & Edited by
David W. Barber
Better Than It Sounds
A Dictionary of Humorous Musical Quotations
isbn 0-920151-22-1

How to Stay Awake
During Anybody's Second Movement
by David E. Walden
cartoons by Mike Duncan
preface by Charlie Farquharson
isbn 0-920151-20-5

How To Listen To Modern Music
Without Earplugs
by David E. Walden
cartoons by Mike Duncan
foreword by Bramwell Tovey
isbn 0-920151-31-0

The Thing I've Played With the Most
Professor Anthon E. Darling Discusses
His Favourite Instrument
by David E. Walden
cartoons by Mike Duncan
foreword by Mabel May Squinnge, B.O.
isbn 0-920151-35-3

More Lives of the Great Composers
From Handel to Grainger
by Basil Howitt
isbn 0-920151-36-1

Love Lives of the Great Composers
From Gesualdo to Wagner
by Basil Howitt
isbn 0-920151-18-3

The Composers
A Hystery of Music
by Kevin Reeves
preface by Daniel Taylor
isbn 0-920151-29-9

1812 And All That
A Concise History of Music from 30.000 BC
to the Millennium
by Lawrence Leonard,
cartoons by Emma Bebbington
isbn 0-920151-33-7

Opera Antics & Annecdotes
by Stephen Tanner
Illustrations by Umberto Táccola
preface by David W. Barber
isbn 0-920151-32-9

A Working Musician's Joke Book
by Daniel G. Theaker, cartoons by Mike Freen
preface by David W. Barber
isbn 0-920151-23-X

Note from the Publisher

I would like to thank David Barber, Dave Donald & Kevin Reeves for all their creative work and support over the years.

Sound And Vision books may be purchased for educational or promotional use or for special sales. If you have any comments on this book or any other books we publish, or if you would like a information about our books, please contact us at 359 Riverdale Avenue, Toronto, Canada M4J 1A4 or our Web site at: http://www.soundandvision.com.

We are looking for original books to publish. If you have an idea or manuscript that is in the genre of musical humour including educational themes, please contact us.

Thank you for purchasing or borrowing this book.

Geoff Savage *Publisher*